From Humboldt To Kodiak
1886 - 1895

Alaska History, No. 40

From Humboldt To Kodiak 1886—1895

**Recollections of a Frontier Childhood
and the Founding of the First American School
and the Baptist Mission at Kodiak, Alaska**

FRED ROSCOE

Edited by Stanley N. Roscoe

THE LIMESTONE PRESS
Kingston, Ontario : Fairbanks, Alaska
1992

Alaska History No. 40

Series Editor: Richard A. Pierce

THE LIMESTONE PRESS
P.O. Box 1604
Kingston, Ontario
Canada K7L 5C8

U.S. Office:
THE LIMESTONE PRESS
History Department
University of Alaska-Fairbanks
AK 99775

DISTRIBUTED BY

THE UNIVERSITY OF ALASKA PRESS
University of Alaska-Fairbanks
AK 99775
(907) 474-6389

ILLIANA LIMITED
2750 Sunny Grove Avenue
Arcata, CA 95521
(707) 839-1271

KODIAK BAPTIST MISSION
1944 Rezanof Drive East
Kodiak, AK 99615-6992
(907) 486-4126

Formatted by Jean LaRoche, Montreal, Quebec, Canada.
Printed in the USA by BookCrafters, Chelsea, Michigan.

Dedicated To

Ida and Ernest

CONTENTS

ILLUSTRATIONS

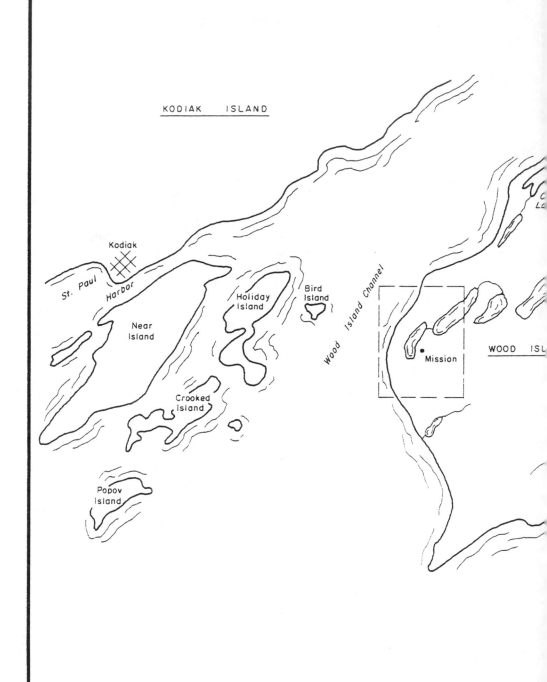

KODIAK   ISLAND

Kodiak

St. Paul

Harbor

Near
Island

Holiday
Island

Bird
Island

Wood Island Channel

Crooked
Island

Mission

WOOD ISL

Popov
Island

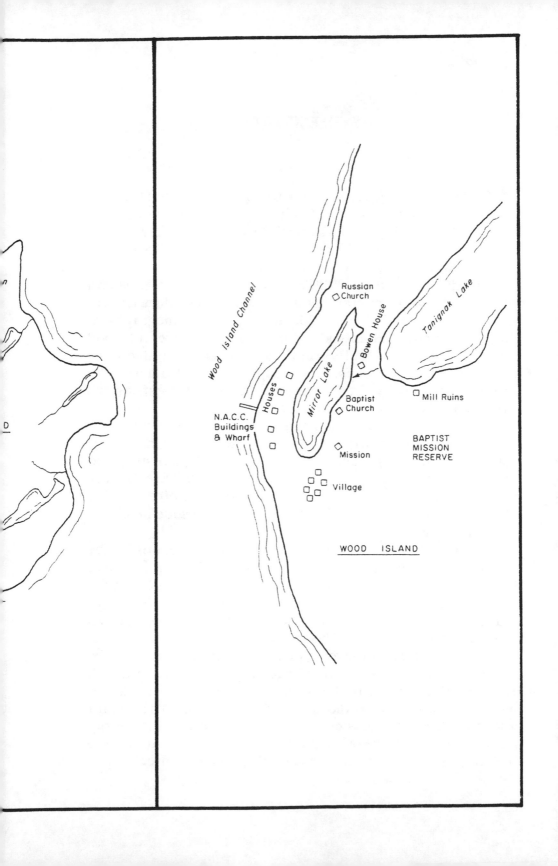

Wood Island Channel

Russian Church

Bowen House

Tanignak Lake

Houses

Mirror Lake

Baptist Church

Mill Ruins

N.A.C.C. Buildings & Wharf

Mission

BAPTIST MISSION RESERVE

Village

WOOD ISLAND

FOREWORD

Wesley Frederick Roscoe was the oldest of nine children, five boys and four girls, born to Wesley Ernest Roscoe and Ida Sophina Dudley Roscoe of Humboldt County, California. His oldest brother was my father, Stanley Boughton Roscoe, so Fred, as he was called, was my uncle.

Fred died of cancer in 1959, and shortly before that he had left a handwritten manuscript with my mother, Martha Beer Roscoe, who died in May 1990. It was an autobiography of Fred's childhood in Humboldt County and at Kodiak and Wood Island, Alaska, between 1886 and 1895. There were also some supporting letters, notes, news clippings, and a few brief accounts written by Fred's parents, Ida and Ernest, as his father was also called by his middle name.

I had known about Fred's manuscript for many years but had never got around to reading it, despite Mother's insistence that it was a gripping story as well as an important history and should be published. So, when Mother died, I read Fred's story and immediately started typing it into my Macintosh, doing minor editing and adding chapter titles and episode headings along the way.

The book is mainly Fred's late-in-life recollections of the heroic exploits of his mother and father, Ida and Ernest Roscoe, as school teachers and Baptist missionaries in Alaska before the turn of the century. There is also an interlude in Humboldt County, California, between the Roscoe family's first and second tours in Alaska.

As for Fred Roscoe the man, he was a stone mason by trade, with an eighth-grade education plus a year at the Craddock Business College in Eureka, California. Fred specialized in fireplaces, but he also did a lot of brickwork on the giant smokestacks of the redwood lumber mills in Humboldt County and the early highrise office buildings that started appearing in San Francisco after the 1906 earthquake and fire.

In 1918, as a sort of vacation lark, he signed on for the season as a bookkeeper with the Alaska Packing Company in Bristol Bay and in 1954 published a fictionalized account of that experience titled *Icebound.* The factual parts of the book are interesting and insightful, but the fictional parts, unfortunately, are a mess of Victorian contrivance. Fortunately, it is easy to tell which is which.

Although *Icebound* is of considerable interest to Alaska historians, it is pale in comparison with the historical bonanza in *From Humboldt to Kodiak,* not only for those interested in Alaska but also those interested in the life and times of Humboldt County, California, in the early days. Few people in their declining years with cancer have written with the clarity of memory for historical detail and the human compassion of Fred Roscoe.

In editing Fred's manuscript, I have retained Fred's accounts of places and events with only minor wording changes to improve clarity without changing meaning. Also, for better continuity and chronological accuracy, I have brought together and repositioned closely related fragments that Fred evidently remembered and recorded at different times during the writing.

I have also included portions of letters and other written accounts by his mother and father, a letter by Miss Carrie Currant, and one by Dr. Sheldon Jackson, General Agent of Education for the Alaska District in the 1880s and '90s, and I have taken the liberty of expanding some parts of the story at the suggestion of his sisters Grace and Helen and his youngest brother Ken. Specifically I have added:

> Some of the names and details of events in the preface, most of which Fred had included at the beginning of his manuscript and the rest of which are in Ernest's written reports (still in Aunt Helen's possession).
>
> Ernest's letter describing Mr. McEntyre's murder and the subsequent manhunt for Peter Anderson (Fred had based his version on later verbal accounts of the events that had taken place when he was one year old) and Ida's personal

letter to Mrs. Hattie Kelsey, both published in 1886 in *The Weekly Humboldt Times.*

Ida's descriptions of the drunkenness and illegitimacy in Kodiak published in 1887 and 1888 in the Annual Reports of the Woman's American Baptist Home Mission Society; Miss Carrie Currant's letter from the October 1893 issue of the *Home Mission Echo*; Dr. Sheldon Jackson's letter from the January 1894 issue; and Ernest's historical description of his voyage to Sitka and back from the January 1895 issue (all of which were provided in 1991 by Betty J. Layton of the American Baptist Historical Society).

Some of the names and details of Ernest's passage to Sitka and back (recounted by Fred with some omissions and minor changes, evidently from his memory of Ernest's verbal reports), taken from another of Ernest's written accounts and from a pamphlet of the Home Mission Society, "Alaska, 1894—1895," by Mrs. James McWhinnie (provided in 1991 by Dorothy Carew of the American Baptist Churches).

Details of the acquisition of acreage on Wood Island by the Woman's American Baptist Home Mission Society (provided in 1991 by Peter J. Ryker of the American Baptist Churches).

Some of the details of the tragic romance of Miss Currant and Fred Haig (clearly remembered and told to my mother in the 1960s by Aunt Grace, who was five at the time of the events).

Fred's false fire alarm at the Baptist Mission on Wood Island (told to me in 1991 by Aunt Helen, who had heard the story many times from Fred and their mother Ida).

Some details of the humorous stories about Rev. R. D. Clark's poor marksmanship, Civil War experiences, and mineral "discoveries" and his wife Seeny's reactions (suggested in 1991 by Uncle Ken, who had heard the stories many times as a child and remembered parts Fred had omitted).

The names and birthdates of Fred's siblings born after this story ends (p. 196) and a diagram of the immediate family of Ida, Ernest, and Fred Roscoe (p. 197).

Despite Fred's remarkable memory for names, events, and places (and his almost error-free spelling of English words), it would be too much to expect that he would remember accurately the spelling of all the names of people and places he knew in early childhood. Also, in the intervening century, spellings have changed. Wood Island has become Woody Island, and the volcanic eruptions, earthquakes, and tidal waves have changed the topography of the lakes and shorelines of Woody Island and Kodiak almost beyond belief. In some cases, I have included the correct spellings in brackets, as I have done with other editorial notes.

A comment may be in order concerning the gradually changing style of Fred's writing as the book progresses. I attribute this to two factors: The early chapters deal with events that occurred prior to Fred's earliest memories. Their descriptions were drawn from family stories and written reports, and some of Grandfather Ernest's accounts were written many years after the events occurred. Consequently, the early chapters do not have the continuity of the later chapters, which deal with sequences of events that Fred well remembered. Secondly, I believe that Fred's writing style developed as the book progressed and he began to feel comfortable reporting his personal impressions of the feelings of others and unleashing his sense of humor.

Finally, some of the words in common use in those times would be inappropriate today, such as "squaws" and "Greek" or "Greek Catholic" in reference to Russian Orthodox churches. It is also probable that Fred's memory of the speech of the Native Aleuts and Creoles was modified over the years by the stereotypic language of American "Indians" invented by the Hollywood motion picture industry. Whatever the case, Fred Roscoe had great respect and compassion for the people he knew as a child and honestly describes in this book.

Stanley N. Roscoe

The wedding of Wesley Ernest Roscoe and Ida Sophina Dudley Roscoe in Eureka, California, in 1885 (photo courtesy of Helen Burnell).

PREFACE

My full name is Wesley Frederick Roscoe. I was born at the Excelsior School District in Humboldt County, California, on September 21, 1885. My parents were Wesley Ernest Roscoe and Ida Sophina Dudley Roscoe. The schoolhouse, where Father taught, stood near the present Miranda School on the old Redwood Highway, now the Avenue of the Giants along the South Fork of Eel River. The house we lived in was near the schoolhouse. Jimmie Wiles and his wife lived nearby, and "Old Lady Wiles" was midwife when I was born.

My father was still teaching at Excelsior in 1886 when he received an appointment from the United States Government to open and teach the first American school at Kodiak Island, Alaska. Dr. Sheldon Jackson, the administrator of Alaska schools, and a Dr. Morehouse, the corresponding secretary of the Woman's American Baptist Home Mission Society, had decided to establish a school at Kodiak. They were looking for a man who was both a Baptist minister and a teacher.

Although Father had not yet been ordained, he had been doing Sunday school work and preaching wherever his services were needed, and Dr. Granville S. Abbott, editor of the *Pacific Baptist,* recommended him for the job. Father was released from finishing the term of school by the Excelsior trustees so that he could accept the appointment.

On June 15, 1886, Father was ordained to the Baptist ministry at the First Baptist Church in Eureka, California. Four days later, on June 19, 1886, the steamer *City of Chester* sailed from Eureka to San Francisco, the first leg of our journey. A large crowd of friends and relatives gathered at the wharf, including many people from the church, who sang "From Greenland's Icy Mountains" to bid the Roscoe family farewell. Evidently that best described their impression of what we would be facing in Alaska.

From San Francisco we went across the bay to Oakland, a small village at that time, to await word to proceed to Seattle from Dr. Jackson. He had already started a number of Presbyterian schools in southeastern Alaska and was in the process of establishing others in the southwestern part to be run by the Baptists and Methodists.

As the General Agent of Education for Alaska, Dr. Jackson had arranged with several missionary societies to cooperate by helping to find and support teachers who would also provide religious services and help to improve the living conditions of the natives. Father for sure and possibly Mother welcomed the opportunity to serve and to experience the exciting adventure.

In August we received word to proceed by train to Seattle, and after a delay in that city, Dr. Jackson chartered the steam schooner *Leo* to take the Roscoes to Kodiak and others to other parts of Alaska. In addition to Dr. Jackson, the Rev. James A. Wirth and his wife were among the passengers. They were to open a school at Afognak Island, a few miles from Kodiak. Mr. and Mrs. Carr were to open a school and do missionary work on Unga Island in the Aleutians under the auspices of the Methodist Episcopal mission society, and Mr. and Mrs. Curry, who were veteran missionaries from Oklahoma, were going on to some other lonesome island to open another Presbyterian school at an Indian village in southeastern Alaska.

While in Seattle, Dr. Jackson had given an impassioned address to the First Baptist Church people, and the enthusiastic congregation quickly raised $700 to go with $500 of government money, which was all Dr. Jackson said he could spare, to send their ex-pastor, Rev. Wirth, to Alaska with us. This made $1200 to support the Wirths for the first year, and after that, Dr. Jackson assured them, both of their salaries would be paid in full by the United States government.

During the long ocean voyage across the North Pacific from Seattle to Kodiak, Rev. Wirth and Rev. Jackson delivered beautifully fervent sermons on Sundays, and Father was called on to offer long and thankful prayers. In one of these, according to Mother's later account, Father "gave special thanks for the memorable sight of the moon rising in the east as the sun was setting in the west, casting silvery tints over the waters."

The *Leo* had auxiliary steam power to be used in case of emergency, but in a dead calm it could steam at only three knots. After a 20-day voyage, during most of which there were rough seas and my mother was seasick, the *Leo* arrived in St. Paul Harbor at Kodiak on September 21, 1886, the day I was one year of age. Evidently the seas had not been rough all the way, for although it was too soon to be sure, Mother thought she was pregnant.

This was less than 20 years since Alaska had been purchased from Russia. Kodiak Island was a wilderness 600 miles west of Sitka, and in those pioneer times, much of it was unexplored, as was most of the mainland. There was no government mail service, no U. S. marshal, and no judge, and murders were frequent.

My father opened the school in a rented building, a cooper shop, that belonged to the Alaska Commercial Company. Mr. McEntyre [also spelled McIntyre], the Company's agent, was very cooperative, and he took a great interest in the school. This building was used for two or three years, during which Father and Mother learned to understand and speak some Russian and the younger Native Americans and Creoles learned to read and understand and speak English, after a fashion.

During this period, Father also hunted and explored over much of southwestern Alaska during summer vacations. A lot of exciting events took place in Kodiak and the surrounding seas, and Mother gave birth to my first sister Agnes in 1887 and my second sister Grace in 1888.

In 1888 or 1889, the government sent up a prefabricated building, with a Mr. Journey to assemble it. The new schoolhouse was completed in a short time, and my father taught in it for two or three more years before we came back to the States in 1891, where Father resumed his teaching position at Excelsior.

A little more than a year later, the Roscoe family, by then including a third daughter, Ruth, was called again to Alaska, from 1893 through 1895, to establish a Baptist mission and orphanage on Wood Island (now called Woody Island) near St. Paul Harbor, about two and a half miles by boat from the town of Kodiak around Near Island and across the strait.

Later fire destroyed the original mission building, and successively the two others that were built in its place, before it was decided to move back to the main island and build the present Kodiak Baptist Mission.

Fred Roscoe

PART I

KODIAK, ALASKA

1886—1891

The village of Kodiak, Alaska, circa 1900. The Roscoes lived in one of the houses along the beach at the right from 1886 until 1890. Wood Island where they lived between 1893 and 1895 can be seen in the distance (photo by B.B. Dobbs, courtesy of the Anchorage Museum of History and Art).

CHAPTER 1

WELCOME TO KODIAK

The Language Barrier

My 23-year-old father opened Kodiak Island's first American school in the fall of 1886. Naturally, pandemonium reigned; the teacher couldn't speak Russian, and the pupils couldn't speak English.

To get around that problem, Father secured help from Mr. Ivan Petroff, the Russian-American customs house officer, who understood both Russian and English. A lexicon was made; words and sentences were translated from English to Russian and from Russian to English. Appleton's Chart and Bancroft's first, second, and third readers were translated both ways, as well as hundreds of easy phrases.

Father studied this lexicon very diligently, then proceeded, chapter by chapter, to drill the children on from 10 to 20 key words from the chapter daily until the chapter was finished. When asked to read the chapter by themselves for the first time, the students were delighted—they could read and understand it so well. Their progress was phenomenal.

The Baseball Game

When the Russian priests heard the children speaking English, they tried to keep them from going to the American school and ordered them not to attend. They wanted to keep the Russian language the language of Alaska. This had considerable effect on the attendance at first. Those children who had American, Scandinavian, German, and other northern European fathers all attended, but most of the others did not.

Father talked to Ivan Petroff about the situation. They decided that a good way to handle the matter would be to start a baseball game at the schoolhouse and have long recesses for a while, until the children were all interested in the game. Soon the boys all loved to play baseball.

Then Father and Ivan made the rule that the players would

have to speak English exclusively. When one would forget and speak Russian, he would have to sit down until the bell rang and the recess was over. When one would forget and say in Russian, "Welee! Welee!" (Throw it here! Throw it here!), the others would laugh and say, "You sit down." This worked, and it wasn't long before the children paid little attention to the priests.

By now all the children were learning to read rapidly, and Father would call them up by name for their reading lessons. Of course Father still got his Russian a little "cockeyed" sometimes. When he would say, "Washka, come up and read," the boy would come up to read, all right, but the other children would just roar, every time.

Father couldn't understand this, so he turned to little Jerry Allen, whose mother had married a sailor. They had lived at Seattle for three or four years where Jerry had learned English.

Father said, "Jerry, what makes the children laugh every time I call Washka up to read?"

Jerry answered, "His name isn't 'Washka.' It's 'Waska.' 'Waska' means 'Willie' in English. You are calling him 'Louse'."

Early Rewards

There were several outstanding scholars among the pupils who first attended Father's American school, in particular Emeleon Petellin, Nikoli Yerocollif, Johnnie Ponfillof, and perhaps the brightest, Antone Dimedof. Here is Antone's record:

Antone came from the mainland, back from Cook Inlet, an 11-year-old boy unable to speak English. In two weeks he could read, write, and spell all the words in the first reader. He soon mastered the second and third readers, and in a year's time he could read *The Youth's Companion* and understand it. He spoke English without a brogue.

When Antone learned enough English to carry on a conversation, he told my father and the children about going out from his house on the mainland with a rifle that a miner had loaned him. He wanted to get some meat for his family and the miner. A band of wolves got on his track. When they got close enough, he said, he started shooting and killed six wolves before the rest turned and ran away.

Antone made this same progress all through school. When he was 15, he got a part-time job in the Alaska Commercial Company's store. He kept on studying and became a very good bookkeeper. Later on he ran the Company's store at Wood Island, across the strait from the town of Kodiak. He became a good fur trader for the Company, and the fur trade was still booming in those days.

After a while some of the younger priests yielded to the pressure from their own children and enrolled them in the American school. Mary Kashevaroff, a daughter of Father Nicholas, was especially smart and became one of Mother and Father's best students [Nicholas P. Kashevaroff was 26 years old in 1886; he was born in 1860 and lived until 1935].

When Mother and Father had learned enough Russian and the students were reasonably fluent in English, Ida and Ernest started a Sunday school. This met with the same opposition. The children who had American, Norwegian, and Swedish fathers all attended, and few others. This too gradually changed.

Justice Served

I can remember my parents telling this story. The episode occurred in the fall of 1886 soon after we arrived in Kodiak, when I was much too young to remember it myself.

Peter Anderson [Andresoff in Russian] was a shiftless, irresponsible sort of person. He lived with his squaw by the Aleut village outside the town of Kodiak. When winter came the year before, he had gone to Mr. McEntyre at the Alaska Commercial Company store and got fitted out with traps and supplies to go hunting and trapping for the winter. He set the traps but failed to look after them and didn't even go to take them up when the trapping season was over. He used up all the supplies but didn't go hunting either. This year when winter was approaching, he came to get fitted out again, but this time Mr. McEntyre refused. Peter Anderson became very angry and left.

That evening Mr. McEntyre, a Mr. Woche, and some others were eating supper in the dining room of the Company house [built by Alexander Baranof in the 1790s; now the Baranof Museum, also called the Erskine House]. Peter Anderson slipped up to the window and fired a charge of buckshot into the back of McEntyre's head, killing him almost instantly. One pellet hit Mr. Woche in the face, but he recovered.

A native boy came running up to our house. He said, "Mr. McEntyre shot; Mr. Woche." (He meant Mr. McEntyre and Mr. Woche were both shot.)

Years later I discovered that Father had written a vivid account of the incident in a letter to Rev. R. D. Clark in Eureka, California, and portions of that letter were published in *The Weekly Humboldt Times* of Thursday, December 9, 1886, as follows:

> A week ago last Saturday Petroff and I were tracking up an enormous bear whose track was two inches longer than my own. Little did we then think that the following Saturday we would be tracking a murderer, but such was the case.
>
> Last Monday evening, Mr. McEntyre, the local agent of the Alaska Commercial Company, was shot in the back of the head, neck, and upper part of the shoulders while eating supper, by a fiend who fired through the window with a breech-loading double-barrelled shotgun. Mr. Wock [Ernest's spelling], who once saved the murderer's life by rescuing him from freezing, was sitting at the other end of the table and received a buckshot just below the left eye and a little to the right of it.
>
> Mr. McEntyre was killed so suddenly that he did not move, and he was finally taken down by Mr. Petroff who discovered that the blood was running out of his mouth. One of his fingers was cut by a shot—he was just taking something to his mouth—and his hand did not even fall to the table. I was called over just in time to see Mr. McEntyre breathe his last. Poor man! I had been talking

to him just a few minutes before.

The murderer was a Russian from the river Don. A most determined search has been made for the man, but as yet he has not been captured, though he was seen to come out of a ravine just at dusk and run across a pasture to an adjacent forest by a boy who had a spy glass.

People discredited the boy's story, [but] Petroff and I took our guns the following morning and soon found his tracks where the boy said he had gone and followed them for over a half mile till we came to a much travelled path close to a house occupied by a man who had been suspicioned of helping the murderer by feeding him, etc. The murderer had taken pains to travel just inside of the paths, in order that we might not notice his tracks.

We have searched every hiding place in town and have searched the adjacent country as well as possible, but without success. We have notified other settlements to look out. As there is no boat or bidarka missing, the man has not left the island.

There are no officers here to look for the fiend, and only a handful of white men. The creoles and natives are good for nothing to hunt for him. They will go with the white men, but they are scared out of their senses, and we are far more afraid of being shot by them accidentally than by the murderer. They are so frightened that they will not go to the woods to chop wood.

We think that when the snow comes we can catch the wretch, as he will have to get food, and he cannot avoid leaving tracks. One man found where a man had been lying down in the woods, but we are more in the dark now than ever. However, we do not intend to rest easy till we have him secured.

We sent Mr. McEntyre's remains home by the *Kodiak,* and Mr. Wock went along to secure medical treatment as the doctor is not here at present.

Two years later, three white men went to another island. When they came back, they reported seeing a wild man eating a crow. He still had his gun, but he was a tatterdemalion; his overalls were worn to shreds, with no legs up to his thighs.

When he saw them, he started to run. They hollered for him to halt. No result, so they fired a shot over his head. He disappeared in the brush.

Everybody around Kodiak seemed to think that was a just ending to the story of the mysterious escape of Peter Anderson.

Mother's Outlook

Mother as well as Father regularly corresponded with relatives and friends back in Humboldt County, California, and on Thursday, January 20, 1887, portions of one of Mother's letters appeared in *The Weekly Humboldt Times:*

Kodiak, Alaska, Dec. 18, 1886

Mrs. Hattie Kelsey——Dear Sister:

Last night about eleven o'clock as we were thinking very strongly of going to bed, I heard a steamer whistle and in a moment more a young man came running to the door and called out, "Steamer," and then was gone to inform the rest of the town. Ernest and I commenced to look for our things to start for the wharf, when he discovered that he did not have his shoes on, and I thought it would be best to dress Freddie before we took him, as he was undressed and in bed: we took him up and dressed him and we donned our wraps and started.

Well, we received over twenty letters, and some of them were good long ones, and it took us until three o'clock to read them, and then I was so excited that I could not go to sleep for another hour, so you see our night's rest was very short. 'Tis almost three months since a steamer arrived from San Francisco. One came the same day we arrived in Kodiak, and that is the last mail we have had, and if it had not been for that terrible murder we would not have had this one. It will be three months more before we hear from home again.

One of the natives has come in, and he talks so much that I can hardly write at all, but he is gone at last. He wanted a Bible. The other evening Ernest gave one of the men that he is teaching to read a testament, so this one made up his mind that he had to have one, too. It took us a long time to find out what kind of a book he wanted. We knew that "konega" meant book, but could not understand what kind of a book. He would measure on the table that he wanted a small book, and finally the thought struck me that it was a testament he wanted, so Ernest went out and got one, and how the man did smile; that was what he wanted, and he wanted to know how many dollars it was. (It was one of those five cents testaments.) Ernest told him nothing, so he got up and shook hands with us both and thanked us time and again, and said that he was going to bring me a sealskin cape for a present the next time he came.

Well, a little boy is now reading. I heard him read a while, and now Ernest has taken him. Ernest has over thirty scholars on the register, but they stay out so much that it makes the average attendance less than twenty. The old priest [Peter S. Dobrovolsky was the senior priest at Kodiak from 1879 to 1889] is very much displeased with the American school. He told some of the men that as soon as the children learn to read English they would leave the Greek church, so he does all he can to make them go to the Russian school which they started two days after E. commenced his. They even went so far as to send a man around to gather the children up in the morning, when they first commenced, but I think we will come out best in the end.

A woman has been in for the last two hours, so I could not write, but when she went away she said that she liked to come for when she felt lonely and discouraged it made her feel all right to come and see me. Poor woman! She does have a hard time. When the U.S. had soldiers here, one of them married her and lived with her a long time, and then deserted her, and now she has three little children to feed and clothe, and has to wash or sew or do anything she can to keep them from starving.

We sit up until eleven most of the time. We are both trying to study evenings, but have so much company that we don't make out much as there is hardly an evening but someone is in until nine. Some of the children in the school learn very fast. Ernest has put several of them in the second reader, and he has only taught school about ten weeks, but some of them don't learn well at all. That is the way in every school either white or black. Ernest is getting so that he can talk with them in Russian some. I understand many words, but can't put them together so that I can talk with them much in Russian, but most of them understand English some, so we manage to get along.

The steamer leaves tomorrow morning and I am improving the precious moments in writing letters to the dear friends at home. You will have a chance to send letters again in the spring, but you must have them in San Francisco by the first of March. You know how eager we are to receive long epistles from you all.

Mrs. Blodgett's Scissors

Mother gave sewing lessons to the native women. They would gather at our home in the afternoon and sew. Soon some of the younger ones got quite expert in dressmaking. They started making dresses for the other native women and were kept quite busy sewing.

The Company would bring up large bolts of cloth of all descriptions. Mother would make herself a dress, and in a week or two a lot of the native ladies would have one just like it—made from the identical cloth. Mother would soon give the dress to some native woman and make herself another out of different cloth and pattern. The same thing always happened.

One day a Mrs. McCloud came to our house. She had a sailor for a husband. He left on a schooner, and she hadn't seen him for two or three years. She said, "Mrs. Roscoe, I've been wanting to give you something for a long time, so I've brought these scissors."

Mother said, "Annie, you can't afford to do that; all I want from you is your good will and friendship."

Annie said, "I want you to take them. I have another pair, and you do so much for me that I just have to do something for you," and she left the scissors for Mother.

The next day some of the other women came to the house. One of them said, "Where did you get Mrs. Blodgett's scissors?"

Mother said, "Mrs. McCloud was here yesterday and said she wanted to make me a present, and she left the scissors when she went home."

The woman said, "Mrs. McCloud was visiting Mrs. Blodgett yesterday too, and after she left, Mrs. Blodgett missed her scissors. She said she'd bet Mrs. McCloud had taken them."

Mother sent the scissors back to Mrs. Blodgett by this woman who lived next door to Mrs. Blodgett.

Runaway Covers

One cold winter night, Father was reading in the library until quite late. Mother had gone to bed and was asleep. When Father went off to bed, the first thing he noticed was that the bedspread and top comforter were gone. He woke Mother and asked, "Idie, where are the top covers?"

Mother looked, and said, "Why, Ernest, they were on the bed when I went to sleep."

Father said he thought he had heard someone in the hall just before he came into the bedroom. He went back into the hall, and the front door was open, so the story was told.

Soon after, one of the native women reported to Mother that a certain native had a spread and a comforter just like the ones Mother used to have.

Teamwork

In addition to teaching the native women how to sew, cook, and keep house and other missionary work, Mother helped at the school when she was needed. Ivan Petroff, Captain Bowen, and some others could also be depended on to help whenever Father had other things to do. They were competent and always cooperative. They all had the true Alaska spirit when it came to helping one another. They all had their hearts in the welfare of the school and the improvement of the conditions of the natives in general.

An American Baby!

The first white child not of Russian descent born on Kodiak Island was the first of my eventual eight siblings, Agnes Ernestine Roscoe, born on May 3, 1887. This was quite an event to the native women Mother was teaching. Some of them and their older daughters were always on hand if Mother needed someone to take care of Agnes and help with the housework. And of course by this time all the women were bringing their children to Sunday school.

The Aleuts and the Creoles

Captain Hanson, of the schooner *Kodiak*, and Mr. and Mrs. Washburn came to our home to visit one night. Mr. Washburn was the agent for the Alaska Commercial Company. He had succeeded Mr. McEntyre, whom Peter Anderson shot. They said that the *Kodiak* was going on a trading trip for a few days and asked Father if he wanted to go along. Of course he went.

I don't know at just what places the *Kodiak* stopped, but they brought back lots of furs. When they were on their way back, off Spruce Island, a large number of whales came up all around the schooner. A 45-70 rifle was fired at one, and the animal was hit in a vital spot. The whale lashed the water and swam straight for Spruce Island.

Within hours, the natives from several villages were busy with their boats, hauling strips of whale blubber to their different villages around Kodiak and the other islands. They cut strips eight or ten inches wide and about ten feet long or as long as they could handily place in their boats.

Some of the smaller strips one native could handle by putting one end over his shoulder and letting the other end

drag on the ground. They didn't seem to care how dirty it got.
Some tied a rope to the strips and dragged them through the
streets. They then fried out the oil from the fat and saved it to
dip their bread in when they ate their meals. Some of the
leaner meat they fried and boiled.

The Company shipped in hundreds of the white bedroom
chambers that were in vogue in those days. The traders sold
them to the natives all over Kodiak and the Aleutians. The
natives used them on their tables to hold their food—whale oil,
fish, and whatever else they had. These pots were placed in the
centers of their tables, and the Aleuts all helped themselves
with their hands to whatever the chambers contained. Many
had no other dishes at that time.

The natives knew of certain small islands where the sea
gulls went to lay their eggs and hatch out their young. Many
would go to these islands in their boats and gather baskets and
baskets of sea gull eggs. They would come back with boatloads.
They would all eat nothing but sea gull eggs until they were
gone. The children would have their pockets full of boiled eggs.
A youngster would take one out of his pocket, peel the shell off,
eat a bite out of it, and throw the rest away; then another, and
another. If you asked him why he wasted that way, he would
say, "Monoga yits" (lots of eggs). After a few days the eggs
would be gone, and the natives would go back on their usual
fish and whale oil diet again.

I have been speaking of the native Aleut villagers. There
were others, part Russian, who did not live with the Aleuts but
had their log houses in a different location. Their living
conditions were a little better, as were those of the other mixed-
race "Creoles" spawned by seafarers of various nationalities,
but in many ways their lot had been served no better by the
beneficence of white civilization than that of the Aleut natives.

Mother's view of the scene in Kodiak soon after we had
arrived in 1886 was vividly described in another of her letters:

> The condition of the poor people is most lamentable.
> Drunkenness is the curse of the country. I do not believe
> there is an adult member of the Greek church in this
> place who does not drink both beer and whiskey, which

they manufacture. The church does not seem to discountenance drunkenness in the least. In fact, the priest and other church officials set the example. The priest [Father Peter S. Dobrovolsky] has often been badly under the influence of strong drink. The people are greatly addicted to petty thieving, lying, etc. Drunken rows are of common occurrence.

You will be shocked when I tell you that about half of the eighty or one hundred children here are illegitimate. One unmarried woman who lives here has, so I have been told, thirteen illegitimate children. Most of the women do not seem to be the least ashamed of their immorality. Dancing is another evil which Alaskan missionaries have to contend with. They think they must have a dance every Sunday night. We do not see the Greek church is doing anything to help these people Heavenward. On the contrary, it is doing all it can to hinder them from becoming enlightened Christian people.

Kodiak waterfront circa 1890, showing the schooner *Lettie* (left) and an unidentified schooner docked at the Alaska Commercial Company wharf. The complex of buildings to the left of the *Lettie* is the A.C.C. store and barn. Above the *Lettie* is the house where McEntyre was shot, built by the early Russians and now called the Erskine House, home of the Baranof Museum. The large building on the wharf is the A.C.C. warehouse, and above its right side is the U.S. Customs House. At the far right is the Greco-Russian Orthodox church (photo courtesy of the University of Alaska Archives, Walter Sobeleff collection).

CHAPTER 2

FREE ENTERPRISE

The Alaska Commercial Company store at Kodiak, Alaska, with barrels of salted salmon awaiting shipment to the United States (photo courtesy of the University of Oregon Library, Clarence Leroy Andrews collection).

The Company Store

As I have already told you, Mr. and Mrs. Washburn succeeded Mr. McEntyre and lived in the Company house that sat on the next bench above the wharf, warehouses, store, and barn.   The store carried an enormous stock of groceries, clothing, and general merchandise. From here all the trading posts of the Company were fitted out, as well as the other towns where their vessels stopped.

Furs from all over Alaska found their way to the Kodiak store by means of those trading schooners and steamers and by other means. The steamers *St. Paul, Bertha,* and others would come to Kodiak and load up with nothing but furs to take out. The fur trade was still enormous.

In this store were huge stocks of red calico yardage and red imitation silk handkerchiefs to sell to the natives at fabulous prices during the first two or three days after they returned from their sea otter hunts.

Of the older generation of natives, none could read, write, or count money to any extent. A large number of the older generation would buy an article and hand their purses over to the storekeeper to take out what he wanted for the article. Then the native would select something else and repeat the operation as long as he had money.

The supposition seemed to be that many clerks took plenty of money out. They dressed their own squaws in red calico and sometimes also bought several imitation red silk handkerchiefs at five dollars apiece, with which their squaws also made dresses.

The Company brought in many suits of clothes.   The natives often wanted to buy the suit the agent had on. It was said that Mr. Washburn changed his suit 30 times one day, as a native bought each suit as fast as he could change to another.

The Company paid the natives from $80 to $100 for each good sea otter skin. Some natives killed as many as 15 or 20 sea otters each trip. The traders weren't too particular, it was said, about what they paid as long as the native village was close to the store, because they would have most of the money back in three days from the whiskey and goods they sold them at outrageous prices. It was said the Company got as high as $700 for a good skin at London, England.

Moonlighting

Some of the white men did a little business on the side. A Mr. Smith sent for a cheap music box and kept it until a schooner load of sea otter hunters had got in and sold their furs.

When the natives had their money, Smith got out the music box and began to play it in the street where the natives were. One native wanted to buy it, and it cost him $500. He played it a while and then filled it with beer and whiskey and ruined it.

Someone asked him why he did that. He said, "Whiskey make Injun feel good. Injun want to make music box feel good, and him stop play for Injun."

The Russian priests were also enterprising. They bought candles at five cents each and blessed them and sold them to the natives for ten cents each, and the natives burned blessed candles in their homes.

We were told by the men in the store that after the natives had spent their money, the Company would trust them for flour, tea, and sugar until they had other furs to sell the Company, as long as the natives hunted for them and made good on the advances. Anything else in the store the natives would have to pay cash for.

Peeva Parties

Cash wasn't so plentiful for them now. To get cash most of them would have to do some work. Many would not work after they got $10 or a little more, for $10 would buy enough graham flour, hops, and brown sugar to make a barrel of "peeva."

The whole village would proceed to get drunk and stay

drunk until the peeva was gone.   Anyone was welcome, including visiting sailors, natives of other villages, and any white man who wanted to drink with them.

One Sunday, when Sunday school was dismissed, we looked down on what the inhabitants called the "Brooklyn bridge," a small bridge across a little stream that ran from the lake to the harbor and separated the town of Kodiak, they said, from the "town of Brooklyn." On this bridge were 24 Aleuts and one Swede.

They had peeva, and the Aleuts probably were a little drunker than the Swede, at least more helpless. The Swede was going from one to the next and blacking both eyes until all had black eyes, including "Andrew Jackson" and "Daniel Webster."

It was all forgotten when the drunk was over, "because him drunk when he did it."

Maxim Punchane, a descendent of the earliest Russians in Alaska, hit Yokoff Yerocollif over the head with a stove poker and put him to sleep for two or three weeks.

Maxim had a peg leg, and a short time after, on another drunk, he took off his peg leg and beat his wife to death with it.

The natives said, "Him drunk when he did it."

B. D. Blodgett

B. D. Blodgett came to Kodiak from Boston, Massachusetts, and was one of the Company's mainstays. He bossed the loading and unloading of the vessels and knew how to handle the natives. He married one of the Chickanoff girls. He made himself useful around the store, bought furs, and tended to anything that seemed to need his attention.

He knew all the Aleuts and others by name. Some he gave white men's names to. One he called Andrew Jackson, others Henry Clay, Thomas Jefferson, George Washington, and so forth. George Washington, they said, was the biggest liar, Andrew Jackson the biggest coward, and so it went.

Mrs. Washburn had a parrot, and the parrot got to be quite a nuisance. When Blodgett would say to Andrew Jackson, "Chuckalooden" (hurry up, in Aleutian), Andrew would look around first to see if it were Blodgett hollering, or the parrot, before he would move. If it happened to be the parrot, as soon as Andrew looked around, the parrot would break out in a big laugh.

Russian Holidays

The Russians went by a different calendar than we. Their Christmas and New Year came at different times from ours. Between the Russian Christmas and New Year, it was a custom of the natives to go from house to house, in bands of a half dozen or more, and sing songs outside their windows.

Each band had a large decorated star, covered with tinsel or other bright material, with a light in the center. They whirled the star and sang. Everybody was supposed to, and did, invite them in and treat them to candy, nuts, cakes, coffee, and whatever was in the house. Some nights a dozen or more bands would come by our house. This continued every night until New Year's Eve.

Blodgett had built himself a very good house with a large dance hall upstairs. This hall he rented for dances, wedding receptions (some of these were very elaborate affairs), and for any kind of a large gathering.

On New Year's Eve there was a grand masquerade ball at Blodgett's Hall. As far back as I can remember, everybody attended this particular dance, whether they danced or not.

They always had a figure, dressed up in the worst rags obtainable, to represent the Old Year. "The Old Year" danced with all the ladies. Another figure was dressed to represent the Devil. "The Devil" had a forked tail. He danced alone and carried an iron poker with a hook on the end. He used this to trip certain individuals when he caught them off guard.

When the clock struck 12, The Devil grabbed The Old Year and threw him downstairs. They picked the same native every year because, they said, he was tough and could stand a lot of bouncing.

After this, "The New Year" came in, dressed in the finest clothing obtainable. He had a good time dancing with all the ladies until daylight, thus ending this celebration.

Dr. Belew

One of the most colorful figures at that time was Dr. Belew. He was doctor, storekeeper, and fur trader. He was considered an exceptionally good doctor and storekeeper, and he had the reputation of being one of the best fur traders that ever hit that part of the country. When Dr. Belew went on fur trading expeditions, he certainly came back with furs.

William Morgan, who was at Cook Inlet at that time, later told me how the doctor did it. Morgan said the doctor took plenty of whiskey along. Also knockout drops. During the serving of drinks, Dr. Belew would put drops in someone's glass. Soon the natives would call the doctor, saying, "Shuska, die!"

The doctor would say, "Show him to me." He would pour a few drops from another bottle in Shuska's mouth, wave his hands over him a few times, and say, "After while he'll come back to life. Pay no attention, he'll be all right."

The trading would be resumed, and after a while Shuska would return to life, evidently as good as ever. Dr. Belew would get all the furs the natives had, then proceed to the next village.

Resourceful Sheep

The Company put 500 head of sheep on an island. They had a cabin, corrals, and some sheds built. They sent two natives there to look after the sheep. During the winter, the natives got tired of their jobs and returned to Kodiak. The weather was rough, and nobody was sent back to the island to take their places.

When spring arrived, the sheep had been given up for dead. Nobody went over to see. The following year, when someone went to the island for another purpose, he came back and reported that there were sheep all over the place. The Company had them counted, and there were more than 1800. The sheep had survived two winters by themselves and had raised their lambs, including many twins.

Their wool was long and needed shearing. The Company needed shearers, and sheep shearers were scarce as hens' teeth at Kodiak. Mr. Blodgett and Mr. Washburn knew Father had sheared sheep in California when he was a boy. They asked Father to help them, and he did.

They took men to the island to corral the sheep, drive them into shearing pens, and sack the wool after the sheep were shorn. Father taught some of the natives how to use the shearing blades and how to hold and turn the sheep to manage the shearing. It took a few days, and the sheep lost a little blood, but Father and his crew finished the job. The wool was taken in boats to Kodiak and later shipped out in a steamer.

Night School

Both Father and Mother had been running a night school for some time to teach the adult natives to speak, read, and write English. They got what assistance they needed from Ivan Petroff. This night school also helped in a great measure to change the vernacular of Kodiak, in a very few years, from Russian to English.

The night school wasn't confined entirely to natives. Anyone could attend and get special attention from the teacher if he needed it. Several took advantage of the opportunity and were helped considerably.

There was an American who sailed small schooners for the Company. He sailed them clear to the northernmost points, yet this man could neither read nor write. Father prepared special lessons for him to study and practice on his voyages, and he soon learned to sign his own name and then to read and write a little, at least enough to interpret maps better and keep a crude log.

The proprietor of a trading post on the mainland came to Kodiak on the schooner *76*. He came to Father and said, "I've come all the way here to learn how to read and write."

Father asked him, "How long do you expect to be here?"

The man answered, "I can stay two or three weeks."

Father said, "That's a pretty short time to learn very much."

The man replied, "Teach me what you can. When I order my goods I have to draw pictures. The last time they sent me a grindstone, and I wanted a cheese."

The man stayed on for about six weeks and then got passage back to his post on another schooner. Father said the man was naturally very bright. He learned how to sign his name and write the names of many articles in his trading post store, and quite a bit else as well.

Father heard from this man several times after that via fur traders and others who stopped at his trading post while traveling through that part of Alaska. They almost invariably mentioned that he had asked them to give him some further pointers about reading and writing. Evidently he had made considerable progress after getting his start at Kodiak. They reported he was reading newspapers and books and was doing surprisingly well.

From time to time he sent letters to Father by traders returning to Kodiak. Father always answered whenever he had a chance to send a letter back. Father saved all this man's letters until our house at Upper Mattole, California, burned in 1922.

Kind and Unusual Punishment

A Russian priest was murdered at the town of Ouzinkie on Spruce Island. The murderer burned the house down to conceal the crime. All that was left of the body were a few charred remains, principally his heart.

A vigilante committee was formed by the people of Kodiak and the surrounding territory. The evidence pointed to one man, Shusharinkin. The committee got this man, and they talked over what to do with him.

Some wanted to lynch him right there, on the spot. They all thought he was guilty by the circumstantial evidence. Some said there was a slight possibility they were wrong.

They asked Father what he thought they should do?

He said, "I think the same as the rest of you, that he is guilty, but some of the evidence is not as reliable as I would like to have it, before sanctioning the extreme penalty. I wish you would talk it over a little more before coming to such a rash decision."

After talking it over a little longer, Captain Bowen suggested that they sentence Shusharinkin to one year's confinement on an uninhabited island, a short distance from St. Paul's Harbor near Wood Island, as it was then called. He could go there in his own boat and live there alone. He was not to leave the island except to come to the store at Kodiak to report and get provisions and return immediately to his island. If he left before the year was up, they would hang him.

This suggestion was decided on by the committee, and Shusharinkin was glad of the verdict. He complied with it to the letter. When he came after groceries he stayed no longer than necessary.

The days and months passed, and on the day the year was up, there was a storm. There was rain, and there was a high wind. The straits were covered with large and rough waves. The people said, "Shusharinkin won't come today."

Mother was home, helping some of the native women with their sewing. They were using Mother's sewing machine. Mother and Mary Chichanof were in the kitchen baking a batch of cookies from a new recipe. The coffee pot was on the stove, and the dining room table was ready for the women to have lunch.

Just as they were ready to sit up to the table, some native children came running and started tapping on the window and screaming. The women ran outside to see what all the excitement was about. The children pointed out to the strait and yelled, "Shusharinkin! Shusharinkin!"

Shusharinkin had a bucket and was bailing water from his boat as fast as he could. He had just rounded the turn from the main strait into St. Paul's Harbor, where the waves weren't so large as they had been on the other side of the point. He could interrupt bailing to row a few strokes before having to bail some more. He finally reached the wharf. His exile had ended.

Petty Larceny

Free enterprise in frontier Kodiak was not limited to the male population. The old Russian priest and his whole family were sick. Mother and the other women were making hot soup, rice custard pudding, and other dishes suitable for the sick. Mother or Father or some of the older native girls would take these dishes over to the priest's house and do all they could to ease their suffering.

This continued throughout their sickness until all had recovered except the priest's wife, who had died while the others were still sick [Anna Dobrovolsky, wife of Father Peter Dobrovolsky, died May 13, 1887 at the age of 50 years]. She was buried in the Russian churchyard, and when the rest of the family recovered, the priest opened his wife's trunk. He told Father about what he found.

He said, "Ernest, I found almost $10,000 in her trunk, from dimes to $20 gold pieces. She had evidently taken them a little at a time, for many years, when I was drinking. I never suspected she was a thief."

The gravestone of Anna Dobrovoisky in the yard of the Greco-Russian Orthodox church in Kodiak, Alaska (photo by Gayle Karshner-Roscoe).

CHAPTER 3

COMING INTO THE COUNTRY

Cook's Inlet and Kenai

Father made many trips exploring around Kodiak, the adjacent islands, and on the mainland. He took photographs and made reports to the Government and also to the Woman's American Baptist Home Mission Society of Boston, Massachusetts. All of the pictures and copies of these reports and many other valuable papers were lost when our family home along the Mattole River burned in 1922, 17 years after our final return to Humboldt County, California. Possibly some of the originals still exist in Boston or in the archives of the American Baptist Historical Society in Valley Forge, PA.

For several years I have kept some recollections Father wrote just before he passed away about their work in Kodiak and his trips with fur traders, but even some of these have been lost. What written material I have, and what I can remember, will serve as a basis for this part of the story.

As an example, in the year 1888 Father decided to visit the native towns along the coast of the mainland around Cook's Inlet, as it was then called. He procured passage on the steamer *Karluk*. The *Karluk* went up the west side of the inlet, stopping at the different trading stations where needed supplies were unloaded, large bales of furs were taken aboard, and more trading was done before moving on to the next station. This continued all the way up the west side until they crossed over to the Kenai peninsula, near the head of Cook's Inlet.

Going up the inlet in a thin blanket of dense fog, they could see the high western snow-capped mountains apparently hanging in the sky above the fog, but they could not see their bases.

Father visited the Indians at all the stops and photographed and reported the wretched conditions at their settlements. They surely needed missionaries and teachers.

These Indians lived largely on fish. One place they stopped, Father heard a racket and looked around to see a ten-year-old boy struggling to shore with a 3 1/2-foot salmon in his net. At all these villages one saw myriads of salmon drying on frames made of spruce poles. The Indian dogs went fishing also.

At the time of the highest spring tides, off the town of Kenai, a difference or variation in sea level of 40 feet is common, Father reported.

Father hired two natives with a three-hatch bidarka [generally pronounced *bidarky* in those days] to take him 16 miles down to Caseloff [Ernest's spelling; now spelled Kasilof]. He sat in the middle hatch and helped the natives paddle, wearing a parka made of sea lion skin, called a kamilin'ke, with strings around the waist tied to the edge of the hatch to keep sea water out.

In Caseloff, Father looked up some friends he had known in Humboldt County, California, and visited with them until the *Karluk* had finished unloading supplies, loading furs, and trading up north before it came down the east side of the inlet.

While there, Father and his friends made day trips far up the Caseloff River. One day he and a friend named Bob Heckman went duck shooting. Father had a double-barreled, muzzle-loading No. 6 shotgun, the best and strongest shooting shotgun he had ever seen. The ducks seemed never to get out of range.

Father would take a whole handful of powder from the powder horn for each barrel, tamp a wad down each barrel on the powder with a ramrod, pour a handful of shot from the shot flask for each barrel, and tamp the wads down to hold the shot in place.

Bob and Father killed a lot of ducks. They slipped up on a bunch of eight king eiders and got them all. As soon as Father had the gun reloaded, two more came flying over, apparently way too high for any shotgun, but the No. 6 brought one down. It weighed more than six pounds. The boys were all in love with this No. 6 muzzle-loader.

They returned to Caseloff with the fine lot of ducks. A trapper friend cooked what they wanted to eat that night, and they gave the rest to other trappers and their prospector neighbors.

The next day, Father and several others went up the river to hunt moose. Father was carrying an armful of guns from the boat to an improvised camp. A terrific thunder and lightning storm came up. He had never seen anything like this! Thunder was roaring all around, and the lightning seemed to envelop him. He dropped the guns and ran off into the woods to get away from the steel.

After the lightning had subsided, he and the others came back out to the river bar where they could see moose tracks all around, but they had no time left to hunt that day. They gathered up the guns and turned back down river, drenched to the skin.

The next morning, Charlie Dudley, a relative of my mother, went up the river alone and soon returned with a fat bear in his boat.

Father visited, hunted, and explored a few more days before the *Karluk* caught up with him at Caseloff. He boarded the *Karluk* and crossed over to Chashick Harbor at the foot of Mount Chernabura, an active volcano.

On the way across the inlet to the west side in fog and darkness, a strong outgoing tide threw them on the mud flats of a small island. Providently, Father said, no heavy wind came up to break up their little ship with large waves. If it had, they would have been doomed, as many other vessels had been in those treacherous waters.

Toward morning the rising tide floated the *Karluk* off into deep water. Soon they were anchored in the harbor at Chashick.

Father went ashore with an Australian sailor, whose name he didn't remember, to explore the beach and a stream that emptied into the harbor. There was a large cliff composed of fossil clam shells. They gathered some to take home, and just before leaving the fossil bed to go up the creek, they saw a family of bears capering over the mud flats at low tide.

When they went up the creek bank, they saw bear trails everywhere and large piles of salmon bones, where the bears had eaten salmon for ages. Some of those bear tracks measured from 10 to 12 inches wide in the mud.

Soon they heard a splash, and looking around at where they had just been, they saw a bear that had jumped from an overhanging bank and had caught a salmon. They both shot.

The bear negotiated the bank and got into the thick alder brush, leaving a blood trail. The brush was too thick for them to follow with any degree of safety, and they lost the bear.

They returned to the steamer for the night. The steamer continued trading from place to place, and in a few days they were back at Kodiak, to my mother's great relief. Mother knew how dangerous Father's expeditions were and that each time he left might be the last time she would see him.

A Dollar's Worth

When Father returned home, one of the natives came and asked if he wanted any salmon.

Father said, "Yes, bring me a dollar's worth."

After a while, here came a lot of natives with salmon. They brought him 100 salmon for one dollar.

He said, "What can I do with so many salmon?"

A big boy who went to school was with them, and he said, "Salt some and smoke some."

Father hired the natives to salt down a large barrel of salmon. There was a smokehouse close by owned by Yokoff Yerocollif, a Russian friend of Father's who lived just above us overlooking the bay. Yokoff smoked the rest, and Father gave him a lot of the smoked and salted salmon when they were ready to be eaten.

Afognak Island

A company was building a cannery at Paramanoff Bay on Afognak Island. The buildings had been framed at San Francisco and shipped to the island where the workmen were erecting them. Father and his friend Crit Tolman, the Deputy Collector of Customs, had been talking for two or three weeks about taking a trip over to the island.

One evening Tolman and his wife came to visit us. Tolman asked Father, "Ernest, can you arrange to get away day after tomorrow? Captain Brown is sailing to Afognak with his schooner, if everything is favorable. He'll be there a couple of days, anyway. He said he'd like to have us go along. The streams are full of salmon and plenty of bear."

Father's answer surprised no one. He thought he could arrange to get away. Everything worked out satisfactorily, and they sailed with Captain Charles Brown.

After the anchor was dropped, a dory was lowered so that the two could go and come as they pleased. The Captain, with a sailor, took another boat ashore to see the superintendent of the cannery.

As Tolman and Father approached the mouth of the river, they saw four bears jumping and splashing around among the myriads of salmon whose tails and dorsal fins were sticking out of the water, bank to bank, literally covering the surface of the lagoon above the mouth. The bears would catch fish as they tried to slither up over the wide, shallow riffle coming into the lagoon.

Tolman rowed around the sand spit at the mouth, quietly skulled the dory along the bank of the lagoon, and landed before reaching the bears. The two men scrambled up the bank and then slipped through the bushes to a point opposite where they had seen the bears. Looking over the bank, they were disappointed to find the bears gone.

Tolman returned to the dory, rowed down the lagoon a short distance, then crossed and hunted on foot up the other side of the river where he thought the bears might have gone. Soon he called, "Ernest," and Father started wading across the river to join him. Before Father reached the other shore, he heard Tolman shoot. Then Tolman shot again.

Father began to run across the shallow riffle and up the bar toward where he knew a bear had charged Tolman. Another shot. Father climbed the bank, saw the bear, and was raising his rifle to shoot when Tolman's gun cracked again, and the bear collapsed.

The bear was draped over a large spruce windfall, 15 feet from Tolman. Tolman had knocked the bear down three times, and it was charging again when it received this final shot. The

A Kodiak bear in the wild (photo by Earl Flemming of the U.S. Fish and Wildlife Service, courtesy of Yule Chaffin).

bear died with its claws clamped hard into the bark of the tree.

Father and Mother told me about going over to Afognak on another occasion to visit Rev. Wirth and his wife for a couple of days. The two men hired a native guide and took a long hike into the interior of Afognak Island. After a few miles' journey, they came to two gorgeous lakes tucked away at the head of a beautiful river.

There were bear trails and tracks all around these lakes. There were trails worn two and three feet deep, where the bears had traveled for ages to and from the lakes. There were piles of fins, tails, and bones several feet high where the bears had eaten the salmon and piled the bones. It so happened they saw only one bear on that trip, but there were eagles flying all around.

The three ate their lunches at one of the lakes, took a few pictures of the beautiful scenery, and returned to the Wirth home late that evening, tired and extremely happy that they had seen this spectacular country.

CHAPTER 4

THE GOOD LIFE

Positive Reinforcement

A year or so after we landed at Kodiak, the Government unexpectedly commissioned Father as Justice of the Peace, and a Constable was also commissioned [the official date of Wesley Ernest Roscoe's appointment as Justice of the Peace for the "District of Alaska" at Kodiak was June 6, 1888]. Almost immediately one of the Russian priests reported a theft of $30 from the church. He accused a certain native and swore to a warrant for his arrest. The native owned up to the theft. He received a jail sentence and also had to work graveling the walk from the street to the church, or serve more time instead.

The jail where they kept this man was a room partitioned off in the Company's barn. There was a good bed with warm blankets, which the man seemed to appreciate very much. His shoes were completely worn out, and Father gave him a extra pair of good boots. Mother cooked his meals, and someone always brought him up to our house to eat. This wouldn't have been necessary, as he would have come alone just as well. He was better off in jail than at home, and he seemed to realize that he was living better than he had ever lived before.

When the weather was good enough, they would let him go up to the church and wheel and scatter gravel along the walkway. Someone asked him what he was going to do when his job ran out.

He answered, "Go steal some more."

On one occasion he had been brought to the house and was busy eating in the dining room. His sister came to the door and was asked to come in and sit down. She was feeling badly about her brother's punishment. She said they had him locked up in the cold barn and fed him nothing but bread and water—no fish or whale oil to keep him strong.

She wanted Father to see if he couldn't do something for her brother, but before Father could say anything, she happened to glance toward the dining room and saw her brother eating a delicious meal. She jumped up from her chair, ran into the dining room, and proceeded to rake him over the coals for sitting there and letting her feel bad for him and make a fool of herself without even letting her know he was there.

White Mama's Food

Captain Bowen's wife showed Mother how to make a fish pie. "Perog" was the Russian name for it, and we all enjoyed eating salmon this way [there are as many different spellings of the word as there are variations of the recipe, including pirok, peroche, piroghi, and pirozhki].

There was an old Indian from a tribe farther east who lived at Kodiak. How he got there no one seemed to know. His name was Arcintee.

Arcintee brought a salmon to our house. He wanted some bread.

Mother took the salmon, gave him a couple loaves of bread, and told him to come back the next day.

Mother got busy and made a perog in a large dripping pan. She used the whole salmon.

The next afternoon, Arcintee came. Mother put the huge fish pie on the table with several other dishes of food. Arcintee ate and ate. He ate three-fourths of the fish pie and most everything else. Then he took a large red bandanna handkerchief, laid it on the table, put what was left of the perog and the other food on it, raised up the four corners, and tied them together. He then went home with his food, happy as a lark.

The other women also gave Arsintee something nice to eat every time he came to their places. He liked "White Mama's" food and lived mostly on what the different ones gave him.

Rhubarb and Berry Pies

Mother loved to pick berries and went berrying with the other women whenever berries were ripe. The wild cranberries were ripe at the time, and Mother and the others picked all they could take care of. These berries grew by the thousands of barrels, and most of them were never picked.

Mother cooked and canned most of hers and also made a lot of jelly. Some of the others put the cranberries down in barrels.

Mother specialized in cranberry pies, using either freshly picked berries or canned berries at other times of the year. Anybody who has ever eaten Alaskan wild cranberry pies, made by a good pie-maker, would pick them over any other kind. They are surely a wonderfully flavored berry.

Salmonberries were also abundant on Kodiak, both red and yellow, with the red predominating. Mother made delicious shortcakes with the salmonberries. The berries had to be picked only a short time before being eaten, as they would turn watery if they stood for any length of time when dead ripe. The salmonberry shortcakes were easy to make, and we had many of them.

Mother and I also picked some Nova Scotia blueberries during their season. They grew on both Kodiak and Wood Island. Mother taught me not to eat berries while picking, or I would never fill my little pail.

There were also a few wild strawberries, and the tame varieties all grew well on Kodiak. Mr. Sargent raised some nice ones in his garden, as did Mr. Pavloff on Wood Island [Frederick Sargent and Nicholas W. Pavloff].

A very few days after the snow melted in the spring, we would get large, tender stalks of rhubarb from Mr. Sargent. It grew in no time, it seemed, and Mother made many delicious rhubarb pies that we all greatly appreciated while waiting for the berries to grow and ripen.

The native children could smell Mother's pies cooking and were always around at the right time to get their share, and of course old Arcintee scored a lot of White Mama's pies too.

In addition to the rhubarb and all the berries, wild flowers were in abundance. A visiting lady botanist gathered and pressed more than 200 varieties and took them back to the States.

Many of the hillsides were covered with beautiful wild roses.

A Close Call

On September 1, 1888, my second sister, Nina Grace, was born at Kodiak Island. Grace, as she was called, was the second white child not of Russian descent born at Kodiak. Dr. Dean, the Alaska Commercial Company doctor at that time, was the attending physician. This was considered another great event by the native women. They constantly called to see the new baby. Mrs. Allen, a native woman, came daytimes to work at our house. Some of the native girls were always glad to come and help, as were the few other American women on Kodiak.

The baby grew and was doing very well until she was more than a year old. An epidemic of dysentery was going around, and the baby caught it. Dr. Dean came every day and sometimes oftener. He thought he wasn't going to be able to pull her through. Finally she took a turn for the better. One of the first things that he prescribed to feed her was a small piece of bacon, fried crisp. This, with the rest of her diet, which he limited to a very small amount at first, was continued until she was well again.

The Christmas Tree

Christmas was drawing near. Father and Mother decorated a tree at the schoolhouse and started preparing a Christmas program. They taught the children pieces to speak and songs to sing. The children loved this and learned quickly with great anticipation.

All the Company's men and their wives, the men and women from the customs house, and the seafaring men of all nationalities who happened to be in Kodiak at the time helped in various ways to make the celebration a success. The Company's store donated candy, nuts, popcorn, and cookies for the occasion. Everybody who could donated toys and clothes for the children and presents for the adult natives, including a large box of warm clothing from the Woman's American Baptist Home Mission Society of Boston, as well as a little something for everybody else present.

Mr. Pavloff from nearby Wood Island was married to a native woman. He was a 3 or 4 priest in the Russian Church. [Nicholas W. Pavloff was a historically important resident of Wood Island for many years, but the author was mistaken in calling Pavloff a priest; the numbers "3 or 4" may have referred to the fact that Pavloff sang the third or fourth psalmist parts in the Greco-Russian Orthodox Church services, and because he wore the robes of a lay reader, the author as a child thought that made Pavloff a priest.]

Mr. Pavloff had been raised in the Russian River Colony in California and was very friendly to Americans, so Father invited him and his large family over for the Christmas tree party. They came, stayed all night, and went home by daylight, across the strait, the next day.

Mr. Pavloff could speak English very well and helped lead the singing. He had a good voice and knew the American hymns and many popular songs. Father asked him where he had learned them.

He answered, "At Russian River, Ernest, when I was a boy. Some Americans had a Sunday school there, and my parents let me go."

Pavloff frequently came to Father's American Sunday school after that and always helped by leading the singing.

Nature's Delicacies

Ivan Petroff came over for supper. He said to Father, "Ernest, what do you think about going duck hunting out on the straits tomorrow?"

Mother said, "Why don't you go after some of those ptarmigan others have been bringing into town lately?"

"I'd just as leave go after ptarmigan, Ida," Petroff replied.

The next morning Petroff came over, and he and Father went back in the hills where the ptarmigan were. They hunted

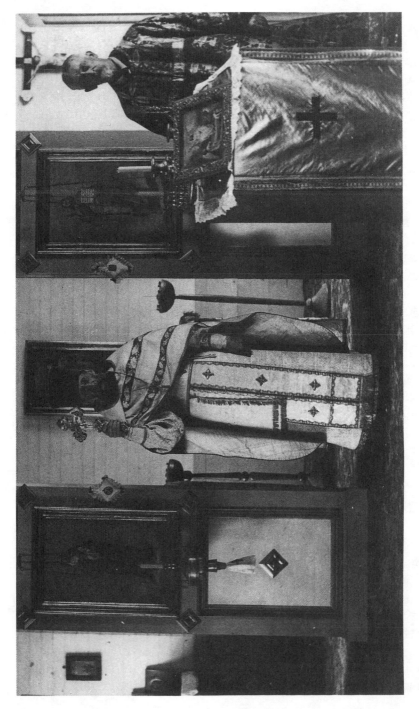

Father Nicholas P. Kashevaroff and psalmist Nicholas W. Pavloff in the Russian Orthodox church at Wood Island in the 1880s (photo courtesy of Dorothy Holm via Yule Chaffin).

all day and got back just as it was getting dark. They had only about a dozen for all their day's hunt.

Father was quite a bit younger than Petroff and stood the hike well, but Petroff was fagged. He sat down in a chair and said, "I'll be all right as soon as I have a cup of Ida's tea."

Mother poured him some tea. He drank it. The stimulant immediately took effect. Father and Mother remarked afterward that they had not known before what a powerful stimulant tea is.

The ptarmigan were delicious, but because there were so few, Mother and Father went down to the beach a day or two later and dug a lot of razorback clams. They dug enough for the family and also for several of our neighbors.

Among our neighbors were Yokoff Yerocollif and his wife. Yokoff was a Russian ship carpenter and a good one. He could make anything out of wood. He worked full-time for the Alaska Commercial Company—repairing ships, making boats, keeping the wharf in shape, and so on.

I was a small boy, but I can remember going up to Yokoff's house when the family was eating whale meat. Yokoff asked me if I liked whale steak.

I said, "I don't know."

Yokoff told his wife to give me some on a plate. I ate it and said I liked it. That was the first and last piece of whale meat I ever ate.

Heavy Pebbles

It was the dead of winter when ships, let alone open boats, seldom ventured very far out on the open sea. The weather had been wild, a big storm had just subsided, and more bad weather was expected at any time.

Several white trappers started from Cook's Inlet in an open sea-otter boat to the town of Kodiak. They put up sail and managed to cross Shelikof Strait—80 miles of rough water. Then, in rounding the island, they landed at a small inlet to get fresh water and camp overnight or, if another storm came up, until the weather would permit them to continue.

Now, on that part of the island, the mountains run straight up from the beach. Right before the trappers was a beautiful waterfall coming down from high up the mountainside. They went to its base and discovered that the water, hitting on a large rock shelf at the bottom, had washed out a sizeable basin. In the central portion of this basin were a lot of pebbles.

These men were not miners, but nevertheless they were curious. They raked some of the little rocks out of the bottom of the pool. The rocks were unusually heavy, and their surfaces were corroded. The men thought the pebbles might be gold, but they also realized that they could be copper or some other metal. One of the men cut one leg off his overalls and tied a cord around the bottom. The others raked all the little rocks out of the pool and put them in the pant leg. Another piece of cord was tied around the top.

When the trappers reached St. Paul Harbor and landed at the wharf at Kodiak, there was considerable excitement. The townspeople were amazed that an open boat could survive the rough and squally Shelikof Strait and continue around the island.

They were excited, also, about the heavy pebbles in the overall leg. Some were sure they were gold; some weren't quite so sure. There were no vessels coming to Kodiak this time of year, so everybody would have to wait until spring or early summer to be sure. When a ship finally came, the little rocks were carried aboard and tested, and word came back that the pebbles were indeed gold nuggets.

Soon there was considerable prospecting around the island, but we never heard of anybody "striking it rich." Some would bring in a little gold, but never any great amount.

Ermine Wraps

Some of the Aleuts from the villages were running steel trap lines and having considerable success. They would return to their villages with a number of furs which they would stretch and cure. They would also tan some if they wanted to make garments for their own people.

In addition to the traps, which caught a variety of fur bearing animals, the natives would often set deadfalls for the little ermine. Ermine were quite plentiful in certain parts of Kodiak Island, and also on some of the other large islands. The natives often tanned these little furs and made beautiful coats called parkas. The furs were white as the driven snow, with a little tip of jet black on the ends of the tails.

After the tiny pelts were tanned fur-side-in, they were turned fur-side-out and sewed together, tails down, like shingles lapping over each lower row, clear around, from bottom to top of the coat. Many wore these beautiful parkas whenever the weather was cold, which was much of the year.

In the summer, a few tourists would usually take passage to Kodiak from Seattle or San Francisco on the steamers *Bertha, St. Paul,* and others. Some of the tourists would fall in love with the beautiful parkas they might happen to see while visiting the villages. Occasionally tourists would buy them, and of course when they got back to their steamer, they would try them on and wear them for a while.

Soon they would begin to itch and feel very uncomfortable until they discovered and removed the cause of this itchy feeling. The parkas were invariably full of lice.

The Shootout

Father and Crit Tolman were forever planning another bear hunt soon. One day I went down to the Company store with Father. Tolman and some other men outside the store were shooting at a target. Tolman had just finished sighting his gun with new sights.

He said to Father, "Come and try my gun, Ernest. See the 25-cent piece standing on edge on top of that post over there?"

The distance was about 50 yards. The light was splendid, and we could see the quarter easily.

Father pulled up the rifle and fired. He nicked the edge of the coin, and it spun off into the grass. He said afterwards, "I was laughing to myself and thinking, Crit'll have to do some shooting to beat that."

Someone found the quarter and replaced it on top of the post. Tolman took the rifle and fired. The bullet hit the coin dead center. Tolman was a remarkable rifleman, and Father was unusually quiet.

The Biggest Bear Ever?

Soon thereafter, Crit Tolman, Father, and Mr. Washburn went to English Bay [now called Women's Bay] for their planned bear hunt. A couple of young natives went along. They always wanted to go on these trips, as they knew they would get a lot of good food to eat.

The boys were beating the brush for bear when one suddenly reared up near them. All the men shot, and they had their bear.

They gutted it, skinned it out, and quartered it. They camped out and let the meat cool all night. The next morning they made a stretcher out of a blanket and two oars, and carried the quarters, one at a time, to their sea-otter boat. They also brought home the hide with the head still attached.

I can remember seeing them unload the bear at Kodiak. It looked like the biggest thing I had ever seen. The head measured over fourteen inches between the ears. The claws were nearly seven inches long. We brought some of them back to California with us and lost them with many other curios when our house burned in 1922.

Everybody who saw that bear said it was the largest he had ever seen. They weighed the four quarters and the hide at the Company store and reckoned that, before it was gutted and dressed, the bear must have weighed more than a ton. Possibly it was the largest bear ever killed in Alaska, and everybody who ate the meat pronounced it excellent—much better than the meat of most bears. [None of the mounted bears in the museums around the country has claws approaching seven inches in length.]

Taxidermist Chris Kleinberger admiring his mount of a large Kodiak bear with typical claws (photo courtesy of Yule Chaffin).

CHAPTER 5

THE FUR TRADE

Priest Hanson

Spring was here, and the vessels started coming. One of the first to arrive was the schooner *Kodiak*. Captain Hanson was her Master.

Captain Hanson was one of the most popular captains who ever came to Kodiak. Everybody was always glad to see him. He was entertained while at Kodiak by the Washburns, Tolmans, Caldwells [William, Lydia, and Caroline Colwell], and by Father and Mother, and he often visited my father at the school.

Captain Hanson was scheduled soon to take a load of natives out to hunt sea otter. They would be gone at least six weeks, probably longer. The Government had put a ban on white men killing sea otters. That occupation was reserved for the natives, as they needed it for a livelihood. White men could lawfully take the natives on these expeditions, but the white men, themselves, weren't supposed to shoot the animals.

Nevertheless, it was thought that many did. (As evidence that might substantiate this assumption, I will point to the wreck of the *C. P. White,* on which I will elaborate to some extent later in my story.)

The natives were ready to go aboard the *Kodiak*. They were now at the store buying tobacco and a few things to take along, very few. The captain had a supply of tobacco and other items that he would sell to them at certain times on the trip.

As you know, the Russian calendar is different from ours, and it would soon be Russian Lent. The Russians had lots of holidays, and few natives worked on a holiday. If they were asked why they didn't work, they would reply, "Prasnick" [*praznyk* means holiday], and they much liked holidays.

Captain Hanson knew this, and he knew that if there were good weather when Lent came, most of the natives would say "prasnick" and wouldn't hunt.

Captain Hanson visited the priest and told him that, even though the weather might be good, Lent would interfere with getting the natives to hunt, and he asked the priest what to do if this happened.

The priest said, "They need the money, and we need the money too. If it's good weather, I want them to hunt and kill all the sea otter they can. I'll tell them you're priest on the schooner. Get them up early in the morning and have service. You tell them to hunt if the weather is good— tell them I said so." [Alexander Martysh was the senior priest at Kodiak between 1889 and 1893.]

The *Kodiak* sailed, and the first morning of Lent the ocean was as smooth as a millpond—no waves, only swells with sea otter sticking their heads out all around.

Captain Hanson had a Webster's dictionary. He told us it was the only large book he had aboard ship. He placed it on a table at one end of the cabin and put on a black robe he had borrowed from the priest.

He woke the natives up and told them to dress quickly, as services were ready to start. He said Father Alexander had told him that if he held services, the weather would be good, and for them to hunt sea otter and kill many.

The hunters dressed quickly and gathered in the captain's cabin. Captain Hanson went through the ceremony using the Webster's dictionary. After the service, they ate a quick breakfast and proceeded to hunt. They killed many sea otters that day and every day throughout Lent.

When the *Kodiak* returned, Captain Hanson told us it was by far the best trip he ever had—good weather and more sea otter than ever before.

The natives, when they came ashore, said, "Priest brought good luck." They were referring, of course, to "Priest Hanson."

The Traders

The Company's store, warehouses, and wharf were busy places this season of the year. In addition to the larger vessels, such as the steamers *Bertha* and *St. Paul,* that made trips during the season to bring in supplies and take out furs, there were a number of small schooners (smaller than the *Kodiak*) that were going out with supplies and bringing in furs. Some brought only sea otter pelts; others brought all kinds of furs from both near and far trading stations. Some had traded directly with scattered tribes, and they also brought back a substantial number of furs.

Captain Bowen often went on these trips, both as captain and as fur trader, and there was always someone in reserve who could leave on short notice to cover ground (and water) in an area where they thought or knew someone else was headed. The important thing was to get there first, and the Alaska Commercial Company's men generally did.

Visiting Traders

White and native trappers who lived elsewhere were coming to Kodiak in boats of their own to sell their furs and take home supplies. Men were coming from other islands, some from quite a distance, for their supplies, and sometimes they brought goods other than furs.

One I can remember was Mr. Woche, the man who was at Kodiak eating supper with Mr. McEntyre when Peter Anderson shot and killed McEntyre.

Mr. Woche lived on an island some distance away. He raised goats. He came in a whaleboat, sailed by two Aleuts, with a load of mohair shorn from his goats. This was to be shipped out on the *Bertha* with Captain Jacob Hansen. Woche took back a substantial amount of supplies and also gathered up a lot of reading material—newspapers, magazines, and books. He always stayed a few days and visited with Mother and Father and other friends before returning to his island.

There were others I can remember, a Mr. Darinoff and a Mr. Cherinoff, who came oftener than Mr. Woche. They probably came a shorter distance. These two men were Russians and were well thought of by everyone at Kodiak. Mr. Derinoff wore a buckskin patch over one eye he had lost from frostbite. Derinoff and Cherinoff knew the rough waters and the wild country, and they were able to cope with the severe environment.

Then there were Captain Thomas and Engineer Erskine

who operated a steamer in the Alaskan trade. They were both fine gentlemen, and Mother and Father enjoyed visits from them when they were in port. They often visited Father at the school and were interested in the way the children learned. (Years later, Erskine's son settled at Kodiak, and the son's wife taught in the very same school Father had started.)

Tourist Guide

Another favorite of mine was old man Sargent. He and his family lived up the street from the store, on the right side, a short distance from the intersection with the street that passed the Company house. Sargent was married to a very intelligent Russian woman, and their sons Eddie and Freddie were also bright and learned well at Father's school.

Sargent spent a lot of time around the store and wharf trading stories and conversation with tourists or other Alaskans passing through. One of the questions they often asked was, "I've heard there's lots of good hunting around here?"

Sargent would invariably say, "Yes, no better in the whole world."

When next asked, "What do they kill?", Sargent's answer would be, "They don't kill anything. They only hunt."

The Revenue Cutters

In the late 1880s, the revenue cutters were scouring the waters for contraband and attending to their other duties. When they caught a vessel hunting sea otter without having natives doing the hunting, they would seize and confiscate it. If they intercepted a vessel loaded with whiskey, they would do the same thing.

The Government had started trying to enforce prohibition on Alaska, and the Revenue Marine Service, the predecessor of the Coast Guard, was attempting to do the job with the revenue cutters. I can remember several times seeing a cutter towing in a vessel and being told that these vessels were smugglers that had been seized for smuggling liquor or other contraband cargo.

A Real Sport

A British Lord, the Fifth Earl of Lonsdale, came in on the steamer *Bertha.* He was a real sport, well equipped with guns and fishing tackle. He spent several weeks at Kodiak, got acquainted with everybody, and fished and hunted continually, weather permitting.

He liked company on his trips and frequently invited Tolman and Petroff and Father and the Company men at the store to go duck shooting and fishing with him. They took turns and went with him when they could. They often came back with more ducks and fish than the few local families wanted, so the surplus was always distributed among the Aleut villagers.

Another Englishman named John Wall Smith also visited Kodiak once or twice a year. He ran a trading post somewhere on the mainland and often stayed two or three weeks when he came to Kodiak. He was a sociable fellow and loved to visit and tell tall tales.

Lord Lonsdale got acquainted with John Wall Smith and enjoyed listening to his stories. Smith invited Lonsdale to come and stay at his post and hunt moose and other wild game.

Lonsdale lingered at Kodiak until he killed a bear and then got passage to Smith's post. He stayed there a while, killed a moose and some other game, then moved on farther inland before returning to Smith's and awaiting passage back to Kodiak.

When he left John Wall Smith's, Lonsdale said, "John, I want you to understand that when you come to London, I want the honour of having you as my guest while you are there."

Smith assured him that he would come.

The Homely Woman

Lonsdale returned to Kodiak and hunted and fished for some time before he took passage out on the *St. Paul* [with Capt. E. C. Erskine].

While in Kodiak, Lonsdale was invited over to Mr. and Mrs. Caldwell's [Colwell] for supper and spent the evening with them. The next evening, Crit Tolman and his wife and Mr. and Mrs. Washburn came over to our house to visit. Lonsdale was there too.

During the conversation, Lonsdale said, "I think Mrs. Caldwell is a very homely woman."

Mrs. Washburn said, "I think she is a very handsome woman."

"Yes," said Lonsdale, "handsome and homely, everything looks so neat around her home. She lives for her home."

We found out that "homely" had entirely different meanings in England and in the United States.

Lord Lonsdale hunted and fished and killed another large bear. He hired an Aleut to tan the hide with the head and claws on. The Aleut did a splendid job. Lonsdale took the hide, along with his other trophies, back to London.

Mr. Smith Goes to London

The next year John Wall Smith decided to take a trip to England. He left Kodiak on the first steamer in the spring. I don't remember how long he stayed, but when he returned, he spent a few days at Kodiak and told all about his trip.

He went to see Lord Lonsdale the first thing when he arrived in London. Lonsdale gave him a room in the servants' quarters. Smith ate with the servants, visited with his friends in London and the surrounding area but made his headquarters at "Lord Lonsdale's" during his entire stay. Before Smith left, Lonsdale invited him to a dinner party with the family.

The Fox Ranch

Captain Feeny was another frequent visitor to Kodiak involved in the fur trade. He lived on Long Island about five miles distant, on the other side of Wood Island. As I remember Long Island, it was about one-fourth of a mile wide and perhaps three-fourths of a mile long, possibly a little longer, but the map shows it to be almost four miles long.

Feeny had the island stocked with Alaskan red foxes. As far as I know, he was the first man to raise foxes in Alaska.

I have read articles of the Fox Breeders Association, and they list the first foxes raised in Alaska in the early nineties on an island in Prince William Sound. This was in the eighties, and when I can first remember, Feeny had Long Island stocked with foxes.

The foxes ran loose on the island, and many delivered and raised their young under Feeny's house. Feeny had a man hired to catch fish for the foxes. The foxes would watch for the boat to come in with the fish and would be right there to meet it.

There were lots of shags, ducks, and sea gulls that lit on the rocks of the island. The foxes supplemented their diet of fish with any of these they could catch.

Captain Feeny sold out his fox business on Long Island in the early nineties to the Alaska Commercial Company for $10,000. That was a lot of money in those days.

By way of comparison, a man married to a native woman owned and operated what was known as "The Milk Ranch" at Kodiak. The wife must have died before the husband, as their son inherited the ranch when his father died. Captain Feeny offered the son $1000 for the cattle and property. The $1000 looked good to the son. He sold.

Feeny ran the ranch successfully, and the son was soon broke. The property was worth many times what he sold it for, or so the story was told around Kodiak.

CHAPTER 6

THE WAY IT WAS

A Fine Looking Man

A fine looking man with a wonderful head of curly golden hair came to Kodiak. All the ladies remarked what a handsome man he was.

Father and Petroff as usual were going on another bear hunt to English Bay, and this curly headed man asked to go along. Of course he was welcome, and as usual a couple of natives went along too.

The natives had their Civil War muzzle-loading muskets, which shot either a round bullet or a lead slug. The other men had 45-70 and 45-90 Winchester repeating rifles, good guns in those black-powder days.

The party arrived at English Bay and made camp, had something to eat, and then took a late afternoon hunt. They soon came across the tracks of a huge bear, which they started to follow.

Suddenly the bear jumped out of a hole he had dug in the sand, and with two bounds he was into the brush and out of sight. They followed his tracks and saw where he had come to a vertical bank at the edge of a 20-foot stream. He had negotiated this creek in one jump, as was evidenced by the deep tracks of all four feet where he lit on the opposite bar. Beyond there, the brush was too thick to hunt further.

The first thing next morning, Petroff and one of the natives and this fine looking man went out for a quick hunt, while Father and the other native stayed in camp to have breakfast ready when the others returned.

Soon the shooting began. They knocked the bear down in the brush. The man with the beautiful curly hair ran through the brush to where he thought the bear was. The brush was thick. The wounded bear heard the man coming and started charging toward him. The golden haired man saw the bear, shot, and ran. When he came out of the thicket, his head was completely bald. He had lost his wig.

They all searched for the golden hairpiece but to no avail. The boat returned to Kodiak minus the bear and the wig.

Shopping Chores

The next Saturday after they returned from the hunt, I went to the store with Father for groceries. He was stocking up with a few of the heavier things. He carried home a 50-pound sack of flour and a large ham the first trip. The second time he brought a wheelbarrow and took home a 100-pound sack of sugar, a side of bacon, and a few smaller items. He often made extra trips to the store after school during the week for additional groceries.

The store prices were very reasonable for the white population at that time, but the poor Aleuts paid double for what they bought. The store keepers made no secret of this, and what we saw left no doubt in our minds about it.

Potatoes were shipped in on the vessels, and Father bought part of what we used from the store and the rest from a couple of natives who raised nice tasting potatoes and had some for sale. They had cellars in which they stored the potatoes during the winter, and they welcomed our trade when the fur season was over and they had little income.

Transient Teachers

Nicholaus and Emma Feodorf [also spelled Faodorf and Faordorff in various Baptist publications] came to visit us for a couple of weeks. They had been appointed school teachers for Karluk, a village on the opposite, or northwest, corner of Kodiak Island from the town of Kodiak. The Feodorfs were both of Russian stock and quite intelligent. They were interesting people, and Father and Mother were sorry to see them leave when they returned to Karluk.

Feodorf was a machinist by trade and had worked at the Union Iron Works in San Francisco before taking the position at Karluk. He wasn't very well educated in the English language, but his wife made up for what he lacked in that line. At Karluk, it was said, she did most of the teaching in the schoolroom, and he taught the natives how to improve their sanitary conditions and to construct different things to make living easier.

Unfortunately, the Feodorfs didn't enjoy the life at Karluk as much as the natives enjoyed having them there. I don't remember exactly how long they stayed, but it was a relatively short time before they returned to San Francisco, and others had to be found to replace them.

Chin Deep

Our house was below Yokoff Yerocollif's house overlooking the beach. I had seen Father pull on his rubber boots and dig clams along the beach at low tide.

When I was about four years old, I got hold of the boots and some way got into them. The uppers were turned down at the knees over the lower parts, and I was always tall for my age.

I made my way down to the beach and proceeded to go wading. The tide was coming in, and the water lapped over the tops and filled the boots, and I was unable to wade out. The tide kept rising.

Johnnie Ponfillof heard me screaming, saw me, and ran to the house and told Father. Father ran down and waded out to me and carried me ashore. The water was then nearly to my chin.

Mental Telepathy

A Company trading vessel returned to Kodiak from an extended trip as far north as Point Barrow. It had stopped at St. Michael near the mouth of the Yukon, both on its trip north and on the way back, and it had stopped at every settlement it could along the way.

On the voyage back, the vessel had picked up two passengers. One was a man who had gone up a short time before as a missionary and had become insane. The other man was accompanying him out. This man fortunately understood his job, and the missionary liked him.

While they were waiting in Kodiak for passage back to San Francisco on a Company steamer, Father heard about the deranged missionary, and I was with Father when he went to see how the man was doing.

This man imagined he could send mental wireless messages and receive answers from different places in the States. He would ask people as they came in, "Have you a message you would like me to send to someone outside?"

Some would give him a message.

He would proceed to send it and then would say, "It will take a little while to get an answer. We will have to wait for it."

After a while, he would announce, "I've received an answer to your message," and would report what it was.

He would then say, "God has given me this power to send and receive messages to what we call distant places. He will soon give this power to others, if they will but ask."

Father and Mother had these men to meals while they were there. The attendant insisted on keeping the gifted man at the place selected for the purpose. I don't remember exactly where this place was, but I know it was not very far from the store.

The Edison Machine

One summer when the sea otter schooners started to come back from their six-week or longer hunt with their native hunters, there appeared on the street, not far from the store, a man with an Edison phonograph. The phonograph had about 12 earphones, as the horn that later replaced them had not yet come into use.

This phonograph was placed on a large dry goods box, and 25 cents was charged to listen to each cylindrical record played. Money was plentiful for a short time when the native hunters were paid for their furs soon after each vessel arrived. The natives had money, and their children had money, as long as it lasted. They were spending it as fast as they very well could.

Both the adults and the children paid their quarters to listen to the phonograph as fast as there were earphones available. They would listen to the same songs over and over. In three or four days we would hear the native children singing the same songs as they came along the village streets. They had memorized the words and had the tunes down to perfection.

The Aleut Chief came to the store. He looked at the phonograph. He said, "You can fool these people, but you can't fool me; there's a man under that box."

He was told to look under the box as the phonograph was lifted off. He turned the box over. Surprised to see the empty space, he said, "Devil inside!" He had learned the name "Devil." He would not listen after he heard the first record, but it made little difference to the children or the other adult members of the tribe.

Sewing Machines

The natives were buying a lot of cloth for dresses for their women folks. By now several of the "Creole" women, those with Russian or other Caucasian blood mixed with Aleut and other strains, were beginning to be very good at dressmaking. They were kept busy making dresses for the other women as well as clothes for their children.

Mother's sewing machine was always in use, and Mother was busy instructing them how to make dresses with new patterns.

It was big news when a steamer arrived at Kodiak with two new sewing machines aboard. Now all three machines were busy all the time as long as the current supply of cloth lasted.

Fish and Ducks

Father and Crit Tolman frequently went fishing off the west side of Wood Island, a favorite spot. They took their shotguns along. They kept pulling in codfish, halibut, sculpins, and other fish, and also shooting mallard, eider, and other ducks as they came flying past.

When they returned to Kodiak, they would have fish and ducks for all the white population. The rest was always given to the Aleuts, who came to the dock and carried the balance to their village.

Mother's Class

Mother had a class of adult native women she was teaching to read and write. Some were making considerable progress. She had taught them how to make cakes, pies, cookies, and other fine pastries and always had coffee and something for them to eat while at the house. They would take turns making a cake, a batch of cookies, or something else to eat while they were there.

Mother took great pleasure in what she was accomplishing with some of the younger women, but there were many older ones who were hard to help to any great extent. They had their way of life that they had been used to since childhood, and they wanted to continue that way.

Quite a number had syphilis so bad that they had running sores way into their bones on their legs and arms and other parts. The poor natives didn't know what they had, and they were dying off at a considerable rate.

There was nothing anyone could do for them. The future was with the younger generation, and that was where Mother principally focused her attention.

Earlier, in the spring of 1888, Mother had expressed her view of the situation in a letter to the Baptist Home Mission Society:

> The long, cold winter has passed away. . .We spent the winter quite pleasantly, for we have had better health this winter than at any time since we came to Kadiak [the usual spelling at that time], and we have been too busy

to be lonesome. The attendance in the day school is improving. We have had over fifty names enrolled almost all winter, with an average attendance of about thirty, and they are learning nicely. I have a class of girls afternoons that I teach crocheting and sewing, and evenings we have school for two hours, but often it is three hours before they all go away. I have had some women and big girls under my instruction, but as a rule they learn very slowly indeed.

We have a nice Sunday school, which we began about two months ago. We went to the parents and told them that if they would send the children we would not talk to them about their church, but would simply teach them what was good, and also teach them to sing. Some of the parents thought it would be very nice, and promised to let the children attend if they wanted to. So we give them a nice card for every ten verses they learn, and they are taking quite an interest.

For the children we have great hopes, but we think it will be almost impossible to do much with the older people. They have been taught that to simply be members of the Greek church will secure them life eternal, no matter how wicked the heart is. They think they can commit the most fearful sins, and then confess to the old drunken priest, and all will be well with them. They commit terrible sins, both men and women. We need the prayers of all Christian people.

Weddings

Every little while there would be a wedding of a white man and a Russian-mixed Creole girl. Many of the men were Swedes, Norwegians, and others from northern Europe. Many of them were or had been seafaring men. Some were now following other occupations—trapping, prospecting, carpentering—part of the time, and doing whatever other work they could get the rest of the time. For nearly every wedding of this kind, it was Father who performed the ceremony in his dual capacity as ordained minister and Justice of the Peace.

Old man Cope, an Englishman, ran the store in Brooklyn, the

suburb on the other side of the little creek that ran through the town from a small lake to the harbor. He was married to a woman of Russian descent. She had been married before and had children from these former marriages including two beautiful daughters, Susie and Mary.

Susie married an American who had a responsible position with the Cutting Canning Company at Karluk on the upper side of Kodiak Island. His name was Paul Morrison. Mary also married an American. I don't remember his name, but I do remember Father performing the ceremony.

New Style Haircuts

Lice were plentiful in the Aleut villages, both head lice and body lice. The Company store had hundreds of fine combs that they sold for combing lice out of the hair. The store also had clippers for cutting hair short on the Aleuts' heads. Mrs. Tolman and Mrs. Caldwell helped Mother teach many of the Aleut women to clean up the vermin. They showed them how to use the fine-toothed combs on their heads and also how to get rid of body lice.

I was only a small boy playing with some native children when we wandered into the edge of the Aleut village. There I saw two squaws combing lice from their children's heads and eating the lice just like monkeys in a zoo.

The men at the store encouraged those they thought lousy to have their hair clipped and their heads washed with a solution to kill the lice and nits. The store also occasionally gave away clippers and medication to natives who would promise to use them on one another.

A couple of clerks in the store started cutting the natives' hair "new style" each time. On one, they would cut all the hair on the front part of the head, leaving long hair behind; the next, the opposite. Then on the next, a wide streak short through the middle; the next, a wide streak crosswise; then, a streak both ways; and then, a topknot in the center of the head; and so it went. Each "customer" wanted a new style, and got it.

The Greco-Russian Orthodox church in Kodiak, Alaska, 1888 (photo courtesy of Yule Chaffin).

CHAPTER 7

MIXED BLESSINGS

Innocent Exposure

One Sunday we went to the Russian church, which was Greek Orthodox Catholic. There were no seats for the congregation. Everyone stood or kneeled throughout the services, as they believed it sacreligious to sit in a church.

Many natives were there, including the blind, the diseased, and the crippled. Several were crippled from syphilis, with pus running out of sores that penetrated clear through the flesh, great holes clear into the bone. They were awful looking sights, these poor, downtrodden members of humanity.

These people were all going up in procession during the services and kneeling and kissing the cross—a syphilitic with pus running out of open sores, then a mother holding an innocent child who would kiss the same spot the syphilitic had just kissed, then another and another, and so it went.

One old Aleut woman came up to Mother and wanted to take my little sisters, Agnes and Grace, up to kiss this cross. Mother thanked her and said she would tell her later the reason she didn't want her little girls to kiss the cross.

After the services, Mother saw the old lady and explained things to her as best she could. Mother said the woman seemed to comprehend and appreciate the seriousness of the problem.

The old lady said, "Yes, it would be bad for the little girls to get those sores."

Not To Worry

One day Anna Olsen came over to our house crying. She came in the door and said, "Mrs. Roscoe, something awful is going to happen to our family."

Mother asked, "What on earth is the matter, Anna?"

"Why, Olaf came home drunk and took our holy water and washed his hands in it and threw it out. Someone is going to die, or something."

Mother said, "Don't cry, Anna, nothing's going to happen.

Nobody is going to die from that." This seemed to comfort Anna, and she went home.

The next day she came back to see mother and said, "Everything is all right now, Ida."

Mother said, "That's good, Anna, I'm glad you're not worrying anymore."

Anna said, "I went and told the priest what had happened, and he made it all right. He sold me another quart of holy water for $1.50."

The Deadwood Rule

Mr. Blodgett and Mr. Washburn went to visit the Russian school. Although some of the priests were sending their own children to Father's American school, they were still doing all they could to make the other children attend their school and not learn to speak English.

When Blodgett and Washburn returned from their visit, Washburn said, "Ernest, the Russian teacher has the 'deadwood' on his pupils. He has his desk behind them, so he can watch what they are doing without their seeing him. He has a big stick with a brass knob on the end. When a student is not studying or is into some mischief, the teacher slips up behind him and gives him a whack, saying, 'What tibia' (That's for you)."

This Russian teacher came to Father one day and asked if Father would teach him English. By this time Father knew quite a bit of Russian, at least enough to understand the question and reply, "Yes, I'll teach you English if you will teach me better Russian?"

It was a bargain, and both profited.

One day one of the other priests was talking to Father. He asked, "Ernest, don't you think it is a mistake to teach these people too much? Soon we will have no more sea otter hunters; they will want to do other jobs, same as other men. Then where will our living come from? The Company needs them to hunt. I need them to live. If they don't get sea otters to sell, I don't get very much money."

Strong Medicine

The natives had a steam bathhouse in their village. They had a pile of rocks outside and a water tub in the room. They would heat these rocks in a big fire, take a shovel and put hot rocks in this tub of water, take the cooled down rocks out, and replace them with more hot ones until the required amount of steam was produced.

Everyone who wanted a bath—men, women, and children—would go there, take off their clothes, and enter the steam room. When they had all the steam they could stand, many would run home through the freezing wind with their clothes under their arms. This no doubt contributed to the many deaths from pneumonia.

There were times when there was no doctor at Kodiak, and those who came and went were not always competent. On one occasion when we had a doctor of questionable competence, there was an epidemic of pneumonia, and it struck the native villagers much harder than the townspeople.

Father and Mother did all they could to help treat and care for the sick. They were going night and day, administering aid and cooking and carrying hot food to the stricken. Some of the younger native women and older girls helped a lot when they were well enough.

Word came that a teenage native boy had pneumonia bad. Father and Mother went over to the village, and there was the boy in a small room with the door and windows shut tight. It was winter, and the weather was cold. The room was crowded with women smoking pipes. Smoke was so thick in the room that a well person could hardly stand it.

The boy was coughing and spitting blood. He had a fever between 104 and 105, and the Company doctor had given up and gone home because the mother didn't trust him and would not follow his instructions.

Mother said to the woman, "If you will do as we say, we will try to save your boy."

The woman said they would do as they were told.

Mother said, "Have everyone keep out of the room except

one or two at a time, and no smoking by anybody in the room. Raise a window enough to let fresh air in and keep it fresh. Keep a fire going in the stove, and one of us will be with you as much as necessary as long as we are needed."

Mother gave the boy aconite, an extract from common monkshood, to reduce his fever. She made a hot soup that day and continued bringing food as needed. She pulled him through.

The mother was a most grateful woman. She said to Mother, "If it hadn't been for you fine people my boy would be dead. When I look at him, alive, I will always think of you."

Stronger Medicine

Several native Aleut and Creole women were at Mother's, some doing fancy work, others sewing dresses, and several taking reading and writing lessons. A couple of the younger ones were preparing coffee and lunch.

During their conversation, I heard one of the women say quietly, "Waselia worked hard, earned ten dollars, bought hops, flour, sugar, made barrel peeva. Men all got drunk. Andrew Jackson very drunk. Grandma tried to make him stop drinking peeva. He got mad, hit her on head with big stick, killed her. She buried Friday."

Shooting Dogs

The natives had lots of dogs who roamed the streets and surrounding country. Some of the dogs became a nuisance around town, upsetting garbage cans, slipping into the store and grabbing a side of bacon or whatever else they could eat, and running away with it. Some of the men in the store began shooting dogs that were making special nuisances of themselves.

One day a native boy knocked at the door.

Mother said, "Come in."

The boy said, "Oh, Mrs. Roscoe, Evan's dead. He's been shot. He's here in the hall."

We all looked, and the dog was lying there dead. There was blood all over the floor. He had run straight to our house and into the front hall after he had been shot.

Father picked up the dog and carried him to the beach. The tide was out, and when it came in, it carried the dog away.

A Sight I Can't Forget

Four Aleuts had gone bear hunting. They took their old Civil War muskets, as these were the only kind of rifles the Alaska Commercial Company would sell a native at that time. The white men were the only ones who could buy Winchesters.

Occasionally a native would get hold of a Winchester by giving a white man many furs in return; at least that's what we were told by those who knew.

I'm not sure where the natives went on this particular trip, but probably down to English Bay, which was readily accessible and a good place to hunt.

Wherever they were, when they started to hunt, one native went ahead of the others. A cub bear came out of the six-foot-high grass. The lead native shot and wounded the cub, and it began to cry. The mother bear ran out, and before the native could reload, she tore his head and arms off and was in the process of tearing him to pieces when the other three hunters ran up and killed her with their muskets.

I saw the three remaining Aleuts land at the Kodiak wharf with the skinned and quartered bear and cub and the head and arms and other pieces of the native all mixed up in one pile in their sea otter boat. I was only five years old, but I will remember this gruesome sight as long as I live.

CHAPTER 8

THE HOME STRETCH

The Nelson House

On Thursday, June 5, 1890, we moved into what was known as "The Nelson House." It was a nice frame building for that time, with much more room than we had in the other house.

During the months that followed before we returned to California, many a miner, fur trader, and seafarer made our home his headquarters while at Kodiak. Many times I can remember seeing one or two men coming directly from their vessel, carrying a couple of grips or other baggage.

They knew the door was always open to those who wished to stay, and Father and Mother enjoyed visiting with these men and listening to them talk about their trips and adventures. My folks learned details of the whole Alaska country that they couldn't get from any other source.

Mary Allen was a large girl in her teens. She often stayed at our house for quite long periods of time. So did Ofdotia Brown. Both had American fathers. Their mothers were of Russian and native blood, mixed. [Ofdotia's father was Capt. Charles Brown.]

These girls rapidly became very efficient around the house. They were good cooks, could sew beautifully and make their own clothes, and kept themselves spotlessly clean. Overall they were good housekeepers.

They both loved Mother, and Mother thought the world of them, for Mother's heart and soul were always in her work with these people, and her work was bearing fruit—not only at that time but in the years to come.

Alexander Naomoff, an 11-year-old boy, was a son by a former marriage of the wife of Mr. Cope, the Brooklyn store-keeper. Alexander also made our house his home a good share of the time, and he always stayed when Father made trips to other parts of Alaska. Mr. Cope said he was glad the boy liked to stay at our house, as it was having such a good influence on him.

Gathering Facts

Father and Mother knew that they would eventually return to the States. In preparation for that day, when Father traveled to the mainland and to other islands, he gathered all the data he could: the approximate number of natives living in each native village he visited, the numbers of adults and children of school age, the distance of one village from the others, the ways and means of getting to these places, and any other interesting and possibly helpful information he ran across.

Ivan Petroff, in his capacity as Collector of Customs, had taken an 1880 census of Kodiak and the nearby islands and adjacent mainland coast, and on their many hunting trips together, Father listened to Petroff's descriptions of all the places he had been.

On one of their trips to English Bay, about eight miles southwest of the town of Kodiak by water, Father and Petroff camped in a native hut of brush and thatch, called a "barabara." A Creole who was with them boiled a delicious salmon for their supper and made tea to go with the sundry delicacies Mother had packed and contributed to their menu.

They were quite comfortable that night, and Father said he lay awake for a long time listening to an account of Petroff's travels and adventures.

Gathering Images

Father had a good camera for that time, and he took many pictures of the natives and native villages whenever he went on trips to other places. Mother helped by developing the films and making the prints.

In some villages, the squaws were superstitious about having their pictures taken and would run away when they saw the camera in front of them. Father managed to take quite a number of their pictures anyway.

As a rule, the men of the tribes liked to have their pictures taken. One of the blackest Aleuts on Kodiak came to our house and wanted Father to take his picture, but he wanted his face white, "like white man," he said.

When Mother had developed the picture, she cut a piece of cloth the size of the image of the man's face, made holes in the cloth for his eyes and his lips and teeth to show through, and carefully stuck this small piece of cloth on the film before making the print.

The native was very pleased with his picture. "All same as white man face," he declared, and he proudly kept it for a long time.

Gathering Trophies

A Mr. Warmburg had a mining claim somewhere on the mainland. He was getting considerable gold from it then and had high hopes of doing much better in the future, when he could get better equipment.

On one of Father's trips into the mainland with a Mr. Anderson, they came by Mr. Wormburg's mine and stayed with him two or three days. Father panned for gold while there and brought a small amount home. He said the panning process was quite absorbing.

A Mr. Ledell, a trader, always stayed at our house when at Kodiak on his trading expeditions. On one trip, shortly before we were to leave Kodiak to return to the States for the first time in almost five years, Mr. Ledell presented Mother with several fox, mink, and ermine furs. The natives had tanned these furs to be ready to make into garments.

Mother said to Father, "Ernest, these beautiful furs will be fine for you to exhibit in the States at your Alaska lectures, with your seven-inch bear claws, fossils, miniature bidarkies, native baskets, ivory carvings, and all the other trophies you have been gathering all this time. I will make the furs into garments afterwards."

Decision Time

When 1891 arrived, the Roscoe family had been in Kodiak more than four years. Father and Mother talked over our future and decided that five years would be sufficient. The school was running smoothly and could easily be taken over by someone else. It was time to take the family back to California when it could be arranged.

They resigned their positions, and when the acceptance came through, packed the things they wanted to take back with them, ready for the steamer on its return voyage. I believe it was the *Bertha* [with Capt. Jacob Hansen as Master], and it would go to Seattle this trip.

When sailing time was drawing near, it seemed as if all of Kodiak was there to see us off. The school pupils and the neighbors, many of the natives, including the Aleut Chief who knew there was a man under the packing box that held the Edison machine, and many of his tribe.

These people came and bade us a touching farewell. Many had tears in their eyes, and all hoped we would return.

Old Arcentee was there and said good-bye to Father and Mother. He said to Mother, "You been good White Mama. Maybe I not see you again," and his eyes filled with tears as we went up the gang plank to the deck of the steamer.

The Lecture Circuit

We arrived at Seattle and stayed several days there and in the nearby towns. Father delivered lectures, and wherever we went, the audiences were enthusiastic.

We took the train south and stopped off at Portland where Father gave a couple more lectures—receiving the same responses—before proceeding on to San Francisco and then to Oakland.

When we arrived in San Francisco, we went to the Windsor Hotel. Father had considerable business to attend to for several days. Evenings he gave more lectures at various churches, always to very enthusiastic congregations. Everybody seemed anxious to learn all they could about Alaska in those pioneer days.

The Parkhurst Family

When we proceeded on to Oakland, we stayed with Father and Mother's longtime friends, the Rev. William Parkhurst and his family. The senior Parkhursts were pioneers who had crossed the plains to California in the 1850s, as had some of the Roscoes and Dudleys, my mother's family. Father's father, Wesley Horton Roscoe, was Captain of their covered wagon emigrant train when they came from Iowa to California.

The next generation of Parkhursts and Roscoes were born in the Sacramento Valley near Marysville, California, including my father who was born in 1863. Both families had moved farther northwest to the Mattole Valley in Humboldt County in the 1870s. Mother was born in Iowa, also in 1863, and had come west by train when she was eight years old in 1871 or 1872. Mother and Father met in the Mattole Valley when they were in their early teens.

Homeward Bound

Father presented several more lectures in Oakland—one I particularly remember being given at the old Fifth Avenue Baptist Church.

When Father had finished giving lectures, we crossed back to San Francisco and took passage north to Eureka on the old steamer *Humboldt* with Capt. M. A. Brandt. We had a rough trip, and nearly everyone was deathly sick, especially Mother. Humboldt Bay was a welcome sight after we had crossed the bar and were finally in smooth water.

PART II

HUMBOLDT COUNTY, CALIFORNIA

1891—1893

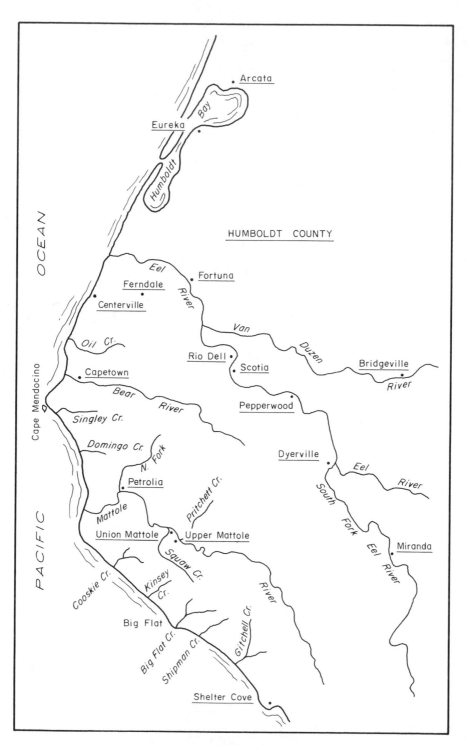

HUMBOLDT COUNTY

CHAPTER 9

A CHANGE OF PACE

The House on Grant Street

When the steamer *Humboldt* docked at Eureka, the Rev. R. D. Clark, who had married Mother and Father, and his wife met us on the wharf and took us to their large Victorian home, which is still standing at 1004 Summer Street, on the southwest corner of Grant and Summer.

Mrs. Clark's parents, the Hendees, owned a house on the lot behind the Clark house, facing on Grant Street and also still standing. The Hendees had moved into an apartment they had added to the back of the Clark house, and the house at 323 Grant was available for us to rent. We stayed there, off and on, for a few months while also making trips to visit Mother's and Father's parents who lived in the Mattole Valley 60 miles south of Eureka.

Father had to deliver his Alaska lecture two or three times at Rev. Clark's First Baptist Church, because the church wouldn't hold all the people who showed up for the first performance. The seven-inch bear claws and the furs, fossils, miniature bidarkas, ivory carvings, and other trophies and curios offered quite an attraction to all who attended. The Methodists and the Presbyterians heard about Father's talks and invited him to lecture at their churches as well, which he did.

Seeny and Roert

On Sundays we went to Sunday school and then to the church services at the First Baptist Church where Rev. Clark was the pastor. He was a good, harmless man, liked by all, and his wife "Seeny," as he called her, was his complete boss.

That was as it should have been as far as financial and numerous other matters were concerned. Seeny had what "Roert," as she called him, utterly lacked—high intelligence and good judgment. Nevertheless, he could deliver a very fine sermon, and if Seeny had any work for him to do, she would write his sermons while he did the work.

The Clarks went with us on one of our trips to Mattole. The Reverend immediately put a shovel and a pick in a burlap sack and headed for the river. He returned with the sack about half full of rocks.

Clark's eyes were ablaze with excitement as he pulled one rock after another out of the sack and declared, "This one is full of platinum; this one is almost pure gold; and look at the silver in this one! I'm going into partnership with the Lord and share the wealth with Him." He hauled the sack of rocks back to Eureka, and neither's share was worth anything.

Rev. Clark liked to go hunting, especially with Father. He had an old-time 44-caliber Winchester rifle and a 10-gauge, double-barreled, muzzle-loading shotgun. He seldom hit what he shot at, but he liked to go just the same.

One day Clark and Father went deer hunting on a friend's ranch near Bridgeville, on the Van Duzen River east of the Mattole.

Father saw a small forked horn buck feeding at the edge of an open prairie across a wooded gulch from where he was stationed. He heard a shot, and the deer bounded off into the nearby woods. Soon Clark came puffing up out of the gulch toward Father.

Clark was excited and exclaimed, "Ernest, I just missed killing a huge elk."

They had supper at the friend's house that evening, and after supper one of the ranch hands came in and said Clark was out in the lower pasture shooting at the mules.

Father's friend asked, "Is he aiming at the mules?"

The answer was, "Yes."

The rancher must have known Rev. Clark pretty well. He said, "Well, that's OK then, the mules are perfectly safe."

Seeny got tired of having Roert forever going duck and goose hunting and not bringing much home, so she filled both shotgun barrels with salt water. When Roert went to get his gun to go hunting, he found it ruined and had to borrow Brother Southmayd's shotgun when he went hunting after that.

Seeny was necessarily frugal, because there was never

much deposited in the collection plates in those days. There was very little money in circulation in Humboldt County. About the only time there was meat on the Clarks' dinner table was when Father or some other church member had been hunting.

One evening Seeny served a large vegetable stew.

Clark helped himself to a plate full. He looked at his plate and said, "Seeny, whar is the meat in the stew?"

Seeny had bought three cents worth of stew meat for that meal.

With Grant Before Richmond

During the Civil War, Clark had lied about his age and joined the Union Army as a drummer boy and was with Grant before Richmond. Despite his terrible aim, he was a brave young soldier, and during a lull in one battle, he misunderstood what he thought was a command, became confused, and clambored over the breastwork and charged the Confederate Army alone.

The Confederate soldiers saw he was a mere boy and held their fire. He was surprised to find it so quiet and looked around and saw that he was alone. He retreated safely behind the breastwork without drawing a shot.

Clark, as did the other soldiers, carried his bedroll tied on top of his backpack so that it protruded above his head and frequently above the breastwork. One night after a fierce battle, he unrolled his bedroll and found the blankets full of bullet holes.

La Grippe

Father's lectures were still in demand in the San Francisco Bay area, as well as in Eureka, so he soon made a trip "down below" to "The City," as it was and is called locally, once again aboard the steamer *Humboldt*. Almost immediately after he left, we all began to come down with "la grippe," as this particularly virulent variety of influenza was called.

To the people in Eureka, the grippe was an entirely new disease that had never been around before. Almost everyone in Eureka caught it, and we were all sick in bed—too sick to get up, and many died. Two of Mother's sisters, Net and Mina, and two of her cousins, Anna and Christa, were with us at the time, and they were all down with the rest of us.

Mother's brother, Al Dudley, and his best friend, Harry Shinn, came in from Mattole and cooked and took care of us. Fortunately, although both caught the virus, as it happened, they did not come down with it at the same time.

Perilous Passage

When Father finally returned from San Francisco, we learned that the *Humboldt* had lost her rudder when crossing the bar out of Humboldt Bay during a fierce storm. The crew had rigged a jury rudder that gave them some control, but the steamer got perilously close to the huge breakers at one point and came near not making it.

When they got out of this tight spot, Capt. M. A. Brandt, whose leg had been broken below the knee, took straight out to sea for quite a distance and stayed out until another vessel finally came close enough to see their signals and towed them on to San Francisco, which took several days.

Some of the passengers censured the captain for heading out to sea and continuing to San Francisco rather than signalling for help from the Coast Guard's life saving station, near the entrance to Humboldt Bay, and having the passengers taken back to Eureka.

A short time before Father got back, word had come to Eureka that the *Humboldt* had been in bad trouble going out of the bay. Mother's cousin, Lincoln Dudley, had heard the news but kept the family from knowing until Father got home—and immediately came down with the grippe. We later learned that the lower portion of Capt. Brandt's leg had to be amputated.

Great Grandfather Roscoe

My great grandfather, Boughton Roscoe, who had come across the plains with his son Wesley's covered wagon train and now lived with Grandfather Wesley and his family at Upper Mattole, came to Eureka to stay with us for a while after the grippe had subsided.

By then I was six years old, and I can remember walking downtown with Great Grandfather to the W. H. Johnson hardware store on 5th and B Streets, I think it was. He bought me a wood chisel to hollow out sticks of wood to make toy boats to sail on the numerous mud puddles in the Eureka streets. There was a dandy on Grant Street just outside our front gate, and I made good use of it.

A few months after Great Grandfather's visit, we received word that he was sick and made a hurried trip to Grandfather Roscoe's home at Upper Mattole. Great Grandfather, who was born November 12, 1805, passed away while we were there, on June 9, 1892, at age 86. He was buried in the family cemetery overlooking Pritchett Creek on the Roscoe ranch.

Another Contract

Sometime after we had returned from Kodiak in 1891, the trustees of the old Excelsior School District, where Father had taught before going to Kodiak, sent word that they would like to have him teach their school again, beginning with the spring term starting a month or so after the first of the new year. Father accepted, and he and Mother decided to give up the house on Grant Street and spend the remaining months at Mattole before going to Excelsior, now known as Miranda.

Moving Day

Mother's brother Al came to Eureka with two large horses drawing a wagon to take us to Mattole with all our baggage and earthly posessions. It was 60 miles to Upper Mattole and 57 to Union Mattole—20 miles to Ferndale, 30 more to Petrolia with a stopover at Capetown about half way between Ferndale and Petrolia, and the final seven to the Dudley ranch at Union Mattole—but with roads as they were and the horses needing rest, the quickest time that could be made was two long days.

That was when the loads hauled weren't too heavy. With the loads hauled by freighters, it took two days each way just between Ferndale and Petrolia, a distance of a little more than 30 miles, or 15 miles a day. With an empty wagon one way and fresh horses, the 30 miles could be done in one very long day.

At that time, the so-called Centerville Road ran down the beach from directly west of Ferndale to the old Flint place south of the mouth of Oil Creek, then climbed uphill for a couple of miles and then down about the same distance to Capetown at the mouth of Bear River. The Centerville Road wasn't abandoned until the new overland Wildcat Ridge Road was completed to the point of being passable in the wintertime in 1896.

A good part of the Centerville Road ran right along the beach from Centerville south. Only the very worst places, mainly the rocky points, were bypassed by grading a roadway up and around the steep hillsides above the shoreline.

When the tide was pretty well out, the road was the best. The people who traveled it then called it a "hard beach." They all liked to "strike a hard beach," and they drove their horses as close to the breakers as they could. The nearer they were, the less their narrow iron tires would sink in the sand.

We stayed overnight at Capetown, "the halfway place," where there was a hotel, stables, and Post Office.

The next morning we climbed Cape Ridge past the Russ ranches—a very steep road with several switchbacks, located much as it is today—then down the even steeper south side of the ridge past the Cape Mendocino Lighthouse to the Ocean House at the mouth of Singley Creek. The Ocean House was the home of the pioneer rancher, Joseph Russ, who owned more land than any other man in Humboldt County.

From the Ocean House we traveled along the beach again,

except for the short stretch of graded road around the hillsides above the rocky Devil's Gate and Morgan Point, to Domingo Zanone's corrals at the mouth of Domingo Creek.

The Devil's Gate was a large rock projecting into the surf that formed a natural archway through which a wagon could pass at low tide. When the graded road around the hillside above the Devil's Gate became impassible during winter storms, travelers might have to wait for the tide to go out so they could drive down the beach and through the archway.

Many years and untold millions of breakers later, the Devil's Gate was pounded into collapse during one of the awful winter storms, but the pile of rocks that remains still bears the name.

As we were traveling these six miles, the wind was blowing with almost hurricane force, cold and cutting like a knife. Sand was flying and filling our eyes. The wagon had six-inch sideboards, and Agnes, Grace, and I lay flat on the wagon bed, close to the sideboard on the ocean side, for protection.

People traveling this beach frequently struck this kind of weather in the winter, and occasionally even in the fall, as we did, but there were also many days when the weather and scenery were absolutely beautiful along that stretch of the Pacific Coast.

From the Zanone corrals, we climbed Domingo Hill, then went down across McNutt Gulch, up over The Table, down through the town of Petrolia, and seven miles over Schenanigan Ridge and on up the Mattole Valley to Grandfather Dudley's at the mouth of Squaw Creek—in time for supper.

Poison Oak

Grandfather Dudley had a sawmill and a gristmill near the mouth of Squaw Creek, just opposite where they lived. He logged with oxen and horses and sawed lumber for the surrounding country. He ground the grain that people raised and brought to him to make flour.

The weather in the valley was hot, and I was all over the

place, from the house to the mills, to see whatever there was to see. I discovered a lot of bushes that had nuts on them. I knew they were some kind of nuts, although I had never seen any like them. I had on a loose blouse that was tight around the waist. I gathered these nuts while crawling through the brush and filled the blouse with them.

The next morning, my eyes were swollen shut, and my face and body were all swollen and itching. The nuts were hazelnuts, or wild filberts, and poison oak bushes were growing right in amongst the hazel bushes.

Mother stripped me and gave me a bath with soda and vinegar and salt in the water, and in three or four days I was as good as before. I have never had poison oak bad since.

Fogbound

Soon thereafter, Father made another brief trip to San Francisco, and on his return, he got off the ship at Shelter Cove rather than continuing to Eureka. His intention was to walk up the beach past Big Flat and then over the mountains between the coast and the Mattole Valley.

Father had known this country—from Shelter Cove to Mattole—very well before he went to Kodiak and had made this approximately 25-mile walk in one day several times. He had known every ridge and creek and trail in this Lost Coast area, every bit as well as he knew much of the wild Alaska country he was used to walking through on his hunting expeditions.

He started early in the morning walking north past Big Flat to the foot of Spanish Ridge, a distance of about 17 or 18 miles. From there it would be about another seven or eight miles over the mountains to Union Mattole, if he followed the right trails.

Unfortunately, as he walked, the fog began to come in. It became so thick that in places he couldn't see the trail he was walking on. When he had climbed what he thought was Spanish Ridge to the top, he started along what he thought was Cooskie Ridge in the direction he thought was north, but after a while the trail he was trying to follow started to descend steeply, and he eventually found himself back down to the beach. Evidently he had come down Lake Ridge, the next one north of Spanish Ridge.

He no longer had any idea where he was along the coast, but he knew he had to climb away from the sound of the breakers. He found another steep trail, but this one also led him eventually back down to the ocean. Evidently it was one of the countless deer trails.

He had eaten his lunch before he started to climb Spanish Ridge, and he was hungry again. So before it would be dark, he walked back down the beach to a cabin he had passed, possibly the abandoned Aldrich cabin, by then used principally by ranchers when rounding up range cattle.

There was nothing to eat in the cabin except a little flour. Father built a fire in the stove, mixed water with the flour, and baked two very hard biscuits for his supper that night.

The next morning, he went out to the mouth of a small creek, probably Randall Creek, and gathered some muscles off the rocks. He boiled them, ate all he wanted, took the rest along for lunch, and headed back from the beach to try the hills again. Unfortunately, the base of the dense fog was still very low.

He started up a steep trail, hoping the fog would burn off as he climbed, but it didn't. When he got to the top where the ridge leveled off, he sat and waited, but nothing changed. He built a fire and lay out all night on top of the ridge.

The next morning, the fog was still bad, but he started out again in the general direction he thought was north, determined to find the trail that led down the side of Cooskie Mountain to Fred Weinsdorfer's place on Squaw Creek and then down the creek to Grandfather's place.

Soon he thought he had found the Cooskie trail, but once again the trail he took led him back down to the ocean, fortunately this time, as he met Philo Moorhead and another cattleman riding their horses along the beach. They hadn't seen him since he went to Alaska more than five years before, but they recognized him, and he was surely glad to see them.

They were below Lake Ridge, about ten miles south of the

mouth of the Mattole River, on their way to Petrolia, which was five miles up river from the mouth and seven miles from Grandfather Dudley's place. It turned out Moorhead and the other rancher had camped at Big Flat two nights before, just a few miles down the beach from the cabin where Father had stayed, but neither had seen any evidence of the other's presence.

The two men in turn let Father ride their horses, while the three walked in turns. They stayed in Petrolia that night, and the next morning, Moorhead accompanied Father to Grandfather's on horseback and led the horse Father had ridden back to Petrolia.

Father had another experience to recount in his lectures.

Grandfather's Mills

While we were visiting Mother's family, I was carefully watching Grandfather Dudley and Uncle Al do their logging, saw the lumber, and grind flour from the wheat and other grains the neighbors in the valley brought to be ground. For a six-year-old, it was a fascinating business.

Both the sawmill and the gristmill were run by water power from the dam they had built across Squaw Creek. The water was delivered through a wooden flume to a 36-inch turbine penstock and waterwheel. The penstock was a 36-inch inside-diameter upright cylinder, with the waterwheel near the bottom. It had a vertical shaft through its center, resting in a bearing at the base and fitting into another bearing over the top of the shaft about 20 or 25 feet from the base. Above the penstock was a pulley, geared to this shaft, on which belts were driven to deliver the power to run the mills.

The dam across the creek backed the water up for more than a mile. In 1891 Grandfather was logging with horses. He had changed from oxen a short time before. There were skid roads around the hillsides and chutes to "shoot" the logs down into the lake. When the logs hit the water, they would float downstream to the mill where they were sawed into lumber.

This lumber was all used locally—up and down the valley for 15 or 20 miles each way and into the hills. With the few and very poor roads at that time (and before there was a wharf at the mouth of the river), hauling lumber from outside the valley was very costly. These mills—both the sawmill and the gristmill—filled important needs of the ranchers and farmers in the Mattole Valley.

CHAPTER 10

OLD TIME RELIGION

Camp Meetings

There were many evangelists, revivalists, and other preachers who traveled from place to place over the country during those early times. Some traveled afoot, some on horseback, and some had a horse and cart. They always got to where they set out to go in one way or another.

A Brother Weber was in the Mattole Valley all of the summer and fall of 1891, and he was at the Roscoe ranch at Upper Mattole and the Dudley ranch at Union Mattole a good share of that time. His headquarters was across the river from the Roscoe ranch, at "Granny" Wilkinson and her husband's place, the same place Father and Mother eventually bought and where my younger brothers and sisters and I were later raised and some of our family still live.

Old time camp meetings were held regularly under the madrone, oak, and pepperwood trees just on the other side of Granny Creek about 150 yards from the Wilkinson house. There were benches and tables galore and a platform for the preachers. Neighbors from Union Mattole and Upper Mattole and farther up the valley would bring their food—chickens and turkeys, fruit and vegetables, and pies and cakes of all descriptions—and eat their suppers and then have their revival meetings afterwards.

There would usually be several preachers, but Brother Weber would always be "the main duck in the puddle." He had a young man with him who had a high, tenor voice and sang the songs that were popular at these revivalist meetings. When he sang, he brought tears to the eyes of many of the congregation and helped put them in a receptive mood for Brother Weber's brand of evangelism.

Brother Weber salvaged many converts, for which he held "baptizing days" every so often. The swimming hole in the Mattole River where the immersion was done was still known as "The Baptizing Hole" by the few who lived in the valley in those days and were still around in the 1950s.

Retribution

During the winter of 1891 and 1892, there were three fierce storms that were generally attributed to the wrath of God, and although nobody seemed sure as to whose sins were causing all the trouble, there was considerable speculation on the matter. Two of these wild southeasters came while we were still at Grandfather Dudley's house at Union Mattole, and one was after we had gone to Excelsior.

On Kelsey's Flat, adjoining Grandfather Dudley's place, the wind blew down 40 or 50 large fir trees. The hurricane-like winds blew the small lights [glass panes] out of the windows of Grandfather's house and blew down his blacksmith shop. Up on Cooskie Mountain, at Fred Weinsdorfer's place, the wind lifted five acres of large oak and fir trees right out by the roots and carried them away. The five acres was cleared off slick as a whistle.

Then the rains came. The river rose up over what was later Senator Way's orchard on the bluff above the mouth of Squaw Creek and backed the creek up over the deck of the sawmill and into the gristmill, which was a few feet higher than the top of the dam. The water was within a foot of the County road between the gristmill and Grandfather's house.

Excelsior

By the time the second southeaster had blown and rained itself out, we were happy enough to leave the Mattole Valley and move inland to Excelsior on the South Fork of Eel River. The distance is not great as the crow flies, but the roundabout route to get there took three days.

Father's youngest brother, Lewis Roscoe, took us by wagon with a four-horse team, which was necessary with the roads full of mud holes and slides from the storms. To go southeast, we traveled 37 miles north to Ferndale, east to Fortuna (formerly called Springville), and then southeast along the Eel River via Rio Dell, Scotia, Pepperwood, and Dyerville, the only towns along the way large enough to have at least one store.

We went directly to the John Logan house about two miles uphill from the wagon road that went through Excelsior. We stayed with the Logans until John and Father had finished hauling our belongings halfway down the schoolhouse trail to what had been a homestead house.

For this job, they used a "lizard" pulled by one horse. The lizard was built from a forked white oak tree cut off below the fork, with each limb cut off about five feet above the fork and boards placed crossways over the forks and nailed to form a pointed sled. This type of sled could be kept on the trail where an ordinary, parallel-runner sled couldn't run.

Even so, it was quite a trick pulling the heavy cookstove a mile down the trail in this fashion, and it took John and Father and the horse a couple days of hard work to get the whole moving job done.

The homestead house had been built out of split lumber made from part of a large redwood tree. The rest of the log was still there, about 50 feet from the house. Father sawed off cuts from the log and split them into bolts with wedges and a white oak maul. With a froe, he rived some beautiful lumber which he made into shelves, cupboards, and a large table. The virgin redwood split like a ribbon.

One of the first things I noticed was a large band of quail near the house. Father made a trench quail trap and baited it with wheat. Sunday came, and Mother made an enormous quail pie, and all the Logans and Roscoes ate this delicious perog variation and visited until evening.

School Days

The next day Father opened the school term. The children were from six years up, and Father taught students in ten different grades in one room, as was customary in the country schools at that time. In addition to the white children, there were several Indian children, some of them from a rancheree upriver. They always carried bows and arrows and were expert at shooting targets nailed to redwood trees.

The Logan children who attended were Janie, Mary, Una, and Simeon. Foster and Arthur had been graduated earlier. As the Logan children walked down the trail to school, they stopped for me, and I accompanied them the remaining mile. We often saw deer on our way, and one morning upon arriving at the schoolyard, we saw a giant redwood that had fallen during the night, missing our school by six feet.

There were other down trees around that had been cut and were being burned to clear the area. The older children built bonfires at noon and during recess, when it wasn't raining, and we would sit around the fire and roast acorns in the coals. The white oak and live oak acorns were the sweetest.

Sometimes children would bring venison, and we would sit around the fire, each with a sharpened stick with a piece of venison on it, which we held over the fire until the delicious buckmeat was ready to eat.

Still No Brother

After we had lived in the homestead house a few months, my third sister, Mildred Ruth, was born on September 19, 1892. Mrs. John Logan was midwife for the delivery of the baby Ruth, as she was called. I began to think I would never have a brother. Who could know that, in the fullness of time, I would have four brothers as well as one more sister?

The Evangelists Return

As I reported earlier, the third great storm of that winter struck after we had moved to Excelsior, and the South Fork of Eel River flooded as badly as the Mattole had during the first two freshets.

When this third storm finally subsided, the evangelists began to appear in the South Fork Valley. Evidently they had wintered farther south where the weather was more temperate.

The first to arrive was the Rev. H. E. Adams. He had two horses and a covered wagon with the name "Gospel Wagon" printed on each side. At first, services were held at the schoolhouse—on Sunday and every night during that first week. This practice continued until the weather was good enough to hold the meetings at the regular camp meeting grounds under the redwoods.

Brother Adams slept in the Gospel Wagon but got most of his meals and his horses fed at the various homes in the neighborhood. People had little money, so his collections were small, but he was well respected and well treated.

As spring started to open up a little more, the roads were drying out from the bright sunshine—quite a contrast with having mud axle deep on the narrow, iron-tired wagon wheels.

As the roads improved, more evangelists and other preachers were appearing. One, a Brother Werst, had two horses and a spring wagon. Brother Burris had a horse and cart, others had a horse and buggy, and some were afoot and caught rides when they could. All were headed for the camp meeting grounds.

They all assisted in the camp meetings and saved many converts and reconverted many who had "fallen from grace" since last year's camp meetings, the extra benefits of which were the joy and comfort of being reborn.

Brother Werst was a Methodist. He merely sprinkled those who wished to be saved. Brother Burris was a Baptist and offered nothing less than full immersion—the only completely dependable procedure.

Some of the preachers would take turns making short tours for a few days to take the Gospel to other "benighted" parts of the country. They would soon return to do their parts in the services at the regular camp meeting grounds where things were better organized and the food and social life were more to their liking.

Sister Weeks

Of course all of the neighborhood people brought lots of food to be eaten before the revival camp meetings, and some took part in the services as well. Sister Weeks was one of these. She not only did a wonderful job of cooking chickens, turkeys, pies, and cakes, but she also spiced up the services.

The evangelists always called on Sister Weeks to testify and then to lead them in prayer when the meeting was at its fervent height. She could testify at great length and put more energy and emotion into her prayers than most of the preachers could.

As for the social life, Sister Weeks always had one or sometimes two of the preachers stay at her house during the revivals. They all liked to be there, for as everyone knew, she was a wonderful cook. Sister Weeks had been raised and still was a Roman Catholic, but she loved these camp meetings and the evangelists, and they all loved her.

Sister Weeks and various other neighbor ladies had offered to do Brother Adams' washing for him. He always replied that he did his own washing and didn't want to bother them with it.

One Saturday the Logan girls were walking down the schoolhouse trail. A couple of hundred yards above our house was a strong spring. On the nearby bushes hung the Reverend's washing. The socks and underwear were made of flour sacks.

Sister Weeks and the other neighbors were shocked to learn that he was in such desperate circumstances. Some scraped the bottoms of their pockets, as money was unbelievably scarce in those days. The donation was given to him privately with the instruction that it was to be spent on himself for things he could best use.

Brother Adams took the money with tears of gratitude in his eyes and thanked them sincerely.

Hellfire and Brimstone

We all went to the revival meetings in the redwoods. At one of these camp meetings, the text was on "Sodom and Gomorrah." I listened the same as other children and adults and was scared stiff about the awful fate that was in store for all those who didn't believe and failed to repent to an angry and "evengeful" God.

The evangelist told how wicked the whole population was, except Lot and possibly some of his family, and how God in his wrath destroyed the city. He went on and on about "the people waxing warm, and then hot, from the fervid heat, till the red hot lava ran down on them like a river and destroyed them.

"But, dear ones, it wasn't over even then for these people. They still burned throughout time and eternity. As the good book says, 'Where the fire is not quenched and the worm dieth not.' Think of this beloved, to be in burning Hell throughout time and eternity. Oh! it is awful to be at the mercy of an angry and evengeful God. Dear ones, I pray for you all to come to the altar and ask for your sins to be forgiven. Who knows, the same fate may be ours if we neglect to seek salvation and don't come to the altar now. God bless you, Brother; God bless you Sister; God bless you my child."

Then Sister Weeks made a prayer about the people of Sodom and Gomorrah and gave all a final warning of their fate if they still defied God.

That night and for a long time after, I had the awfulest nightmares a child ever had. I could feel the awful heat "waxing warm and then hot" from the volcano that was coming down upon us. I could see people scrambling and falling over one another to get out of the way, and the red hot lava running over them all.

When I got a little older and brave enough to think a little for myself without being too scared to think, I got over the nightmares, but this sort of emotional religion left its imprint for the rest of my life.

PART III

WOOD ISLAND, ALASKA

1893—1895

Two views of Mirror Lake on Wood Island, looking toward the mountains of Kodiak Island and showing some of the buildings acquired in 1891 by the North American Commercial Company. The upper photo, taken from the site of the future Baptist Mission, shows part of what had been the ingenious ice establishment of the American Russian Commercial Company (photos courtesy of the American Baptist Historical Society).

CHAPTER 11

A SECOND CALLING

On the Waves Again

Before we left Kodiak, Father had recommended to the Woman's American Baptist Home Mission Society that a mission be established at or near Kodiak, as an orphanage was badly needed there, and Dr. Sheldon Jackson had strongly supported the recommendation. In December, 1891, the Society agreed, and during the time Father was teaching at the Excelsior School, the plans were drawn and the lumber and other building materials made ready to ship out of San Francisco in the spring of 1892.

The first vessel bound for Kodiak that year belonged to the North American Commercial Company, which had started operating in that part of Alaska since we had left. Their headquarters was at Wood Island, about two and a half miles from Kodiak by boat around Near Island and across the strait.

Mr. Feodorf who, with his wife, had taught at Karluk for a short time while we were at Kodiak, went up on this vessel and oversaw the unloading of the lumber and supplies near the wharf at Wood Island, then went back to San Francisco on the return voyage.

Meanwhile, the Home Mission Society had contacted Father and asked him to take the position of superintending the construction of the mission and running the orphanage afterwards, with Mother as matron. Father and Mother had accepted. Once again, the trustees of the Excelsior School District accepted Father's resignation, and we left as soon as another teacher arrived to take Father's place.

Mother's brother, Al Dudley, came with horses and wagon and moved us to Mattole for a brief visit with Father's and Mother's folks, this time in good weather by the shortcut via Briceland, Ettersburg, and Wilder Ridge. After the visit, Al took us on to Eureka to catch, once again, the steamer Humboldt bound for San Francisco. As usual in those times, a big delegation of friends was at the wharf to bid us goodbye.

In San Francisco we again stayed at the Windsor Hotel while awaiting passage on the schooner Kodiak with our old friend Captain Hanson as Master.

As we sailed out through the Golden Gate on March 3, 1893, the *Kodiak* was run into by the *Mary E. Russ*. The *Kodiak*'s bow was laid wide open, nearly to the waterline. We had to be towed back to San Francisco for repairs. In about two weeks, our journey was resumed, and 21 days later we arrived at the wharf in Kodiak, on April 8, 1893.

Welcome To Wood Island

As soon as the *Kodiak* was tied up to the dock, Captain Bowen, an old friend from our earlier Kodiak days, came aboard. He had quit the Alaska Commercial Company and had moved to Wood Island, as it was then called, to work for the North American Commercial Company. Captain Bowen told Father the lumber had been unloaded and piled near the Wood Island wharf and that there was plenty of good government land nearby that could be filed on in the name of the Baptist Mission Society.

Mr. Greenfield, the superintendent of the North American Commercial Company, had instructed Captain Bowen to invite us to the Greenfield home until we got settled. Captain Bowen took us over to Wood Island in his boat, and Mr. Greenfield rented us a log house, which we moved into as soon as we could bring our things from Kodiak. The house was located on the spit between the strait and a lake just back from the shoreline. We lived in the log house until sufficient work was done on the mission to allow us to move in.

The Log House

The log house consisted of one large room with an attic that was reached from the outside by a ladder. Father went to Kodiak and hired a couple of carpenters he knew. The men slept in this attic, and they would also have to be boarded. A curtain was installed to divide the large room, and a couple of shorter curtains separated the back section into bedrooms and a kitchen, where Mother prepared the food for all.

There was a cook stove in the kitchen and a large heating stove in the front room. Both burned coal. We all ate together at a large table in the front room, and after supper the men sat around the heating stove, spun yarns, read books, and entertained themselves as best they could.

Enterprising Carpenters

Now Father began hiring what men he could use to advantage, and the carpenters started building the Mission. Natives carried the lumber about a hundred yards to the lake where a huge raft was made and towed to the opposite shore. The lumber was then carried another hundred yards and racked up so the wind would blow through and dry it before it was used.

The building was barely started when a small two-masted schooner stopped at Wood Island. This schooner had come from Puget Sound, and the three men aboard claimed to have a cargo principally of potatoes, a few onions, and other vegetables. They said these were to be sold and traded for furs, but they surely did not have a whole shipload of produce, and what else they may have had aboard they didn't say.

The three men had built the schooner themselves on Puget Sound. They were all expert ship carpenters, as well as good navigators, and Father hired them to work on the Mission. The Captain's name was Lind, and one of the mates was named Gibson. I don't remember the third man's name.

Soon Father made Lind the construction foreman, and he worked on the mission full-time, but the other two worked only when the schooner was at Wood Island. The rest of the time, they made trips to Cook Inlet and other parts of Alaska with a couple of native crewmembers they hired. There was much speculation, but the purpose of these trips was never revealed.

Around Wood Island, some distance from the wharf and company buildings, was a lagoon nestled behind a hill that was high enough to hide a small vessel from the view of other vessels passing through the strait. Revenue cutters were often in the vicinity searching for any vessels whose purpose in the area might be suspect.

The carpenters found this lagoon and used it for their harbor all the time they were at Wood Island. There was plenty of room for the little schooner, and it was safe from even the severest storm. As it happened, it also was never detected by the revenue cutters.

Taking Up Land

A party of U. S. Government surveyors stopped at Kodiak. While they were there, Father got instructions from them as to how to proceed in taking up government land for the orphanage. They told Father to survey the land he wanted and file the description of the survey at the U. S. Land Office at Sitka.

Father got Gibson, with his compass from the schooner, and they started the survey from an established point near the lake. They ran a line across the island through spruce timber and came out into a large, wonderful meadow with six-foot-high grass. They included this excellent land in the claim before closing their survey line back to the starting point. This meadow would prove valuable to the Mission in producing grass hay for the cattle. Father many years later wrote that the survey had included a quarter section of land, or 160 acres, but the acreage must have heen considerably more than that.

[The 1894 Annual Report of the Woman's American Baptist Mission Society stated that 640 acres, a full section, had been taken up. Subsequently, Curtis P. Coe, who succeeded Wesley Ernest Roscoe as Superintendent of the Mission in 1895, applied for land that he assumed would total 600 acres, and Acting Superintendent Stephen A. Coldwell, in Coe's temporary absence, applied for an additional 10-1/2 acres in the Village of Wood Island. USA Survey No. 626, showing a total of 562.77 acres, was made in 1905 by Frank H. Lascy, U.S. Deputy Surveyor, and that was the acreage officially conveyed as the "Baptist Mission Reserve" in 1942 over the signature of

"Franklin D. Roosevelt," obviously in the handwriting of his secretary, Ruth W. Talley.]

Another Peeva Party

The native workers continued carrying lumber to the lake, rafting it across, and then carrying it on to the construction site and racking it to dry while the carpenters were still framing the building.

The native village on Wood Island was two or three hundred yards from the North American Commercial Company store and somewhat less from the wharf where our lumber was stacked.

Came a Monday morning, and only one native showed up to carry lumber. A new batch of peeva was properly fermented and ready to drink, and everybody was welcome, native and white, from Kodiak and elsewhere, until the whole barrel was emptied.

About the middle of the week, the natives started showing up to work. A new batch of peeva was never started until the last one was finished, so it would probably be a month before another barrel would be ready. During that time, all the lumber would be across the lake and racked to dry.

Out of the Past

On July 4, 1893, a 13-year-old, part-native boy who had often stayed with us when we lived at Kodiak came to Wood Island and asked Mother if he could live with us. He went by the name of Shurka Cope, although his real name was Alexander Naomoff, as his father was one of his mother's former husbands. Mother welcomed Shurkie, as we called him, into our household, and old man Cope, the Brooklyn storekeeper and the mother's current husband, was pleased to have him at the new Baptist Mission. Thus, Alexander Naomoff, alias Shurka Cope, was the first to be admitted to the orphanage, even though it was still under construction.

Shurkie loved to take Father fishing, and I usually got to go along. As I have said, there was a great fishing hole in the strait off the end of Wood Island, and we always came home with a boatload of codfish, halibut, sculpin, and other rock fish. On these outings, Father was never without his locally famous No. 6 muzzle loader and shot ducks whenever some flew over.

In three or four hours we would have enough fish and fowl for the Roscoes, Bowens, and Greenfields, with plenty left over for the native workers and villagers. None was wasted.

Another of Father and Mother's former pupils, their star scholar Antone Dimedof, was now running a store and buying furs for the Alaska Commercial Company here on Wood Island. His trading post was about one hundred yards toward the street from the log house we were living in. Antone had by now become a fine trader, and he often visited us as long as we were on Wood Island.

One day Johnnie Ponfillof, Nicoli Yerocollif, and Eddie and Freddie Sargent came over from Kodiak to Wood Island to pay Mother and Father a visit. They had stopped off at the Alaska Commercial Company store and picked up Antone Dimedof, who came along with them. All had been pupils in Father's school in Kodiak, and all had been frequent visitors in our home during those years.

Of course the folks were delighted to have these young men remember them in this way. They were shown through the Mission, including the schoolroom, and were very interested in what the folks were doing. Mother thought they seemed a bit uneasy as they were leaving, but they promised to come back and visit us again soon, and they would keep that promise.

Many of the other children from the Aleut village at Kodiak would come across the strait and drop in to see Mother. Mother always had cake and pie and cookies on hand, and these children were old hands at eating White Mama's sweets. Of course it was not long before the children from the Aleut village on Wood Island were doing the same, and in the process they soon began to understand some English and to speak it a little as well.

Another Old Friend

The Russians' Greek Catholic Church was a couple of hundred yards up the lake from our log house, between the lake and the strait. Father's old friend, Nicholas Pavloff, who was born in 1846 and raised until the age of 13 in the Russian River Valley in northern California, was still one of the priests there.

As a young man, Pavloff had shipped out on Russian sailing schooners, hunting sea otter, trading, and hauling merchandise both ways between California and Alaska. He later became a priest and eventually settled at Wood Island and married a native woman and had many children [Pavloff was not a priest; recall earlier note].

Pavloff was friendly to all Americans, much more so than many of the other priests in the Aleutian area. He would come to Father's American Sunday school and lead the singing and take part in other activities. As I have said, he was a fine singer, and everybody liked Mr. Pavloff because he welcomed what was being done by the Americans to help the condition of the poor natives.

The Monument

While the Mission was being built, I got to know the children in the Aleut village and played with them a lot. A short distance southwest of this village was their cemetery. There were quite a number of graves marked by a stick driven at the head of the grave and another at the foot.

I have no way of knowing whether it had always been an Aleut cemetery, but one grave was different from all the rest and attracted my close attention. Whose grave could it have been? Possibly a high up chief, or more likely, perhaps, an early Russian of great influence? I do not know.

At the head of this grave was the most picturesque monument, and I venture to say, figured in terms of days of labor by expert wood carvers, it must have been the most costly in all of Alaska. Kodiak and Wood Island were not in the totem pole area, so the artisans had to be imported, and I believe this piece of work beat them all.

My memory tells me that the base of this monument must have been at least 12 feet square and 8 feet high. The die, or upper part of the work of art, was made from a giant spruce tree carved into the most hideous looking creature any imagination could conceive.

It was at least 60 feet in length. Its huge, supremely fascinating, hideous head, full chest, and two alligator-like arms were resting above this huge base on two immense wood-carved hands. The body tapered as it ran back to form the tail of this monster. The carvings all along the body were in keeping with the rest of this splendid piece of work.

Mysterious Lakes

Mr. Greenfield had loaned Father a boat to use in crossing the lake, but that was only a temporary arrangement. Mr. Lind, the master ship carpenter, volunteered to build Father a boat to cross the lake in if Father would arrange to get the right lumber from the Company. Father got the lumber, and Lind did the work in the Company's shop. I often rode across the lake with the men when they went to work in the new boat and then walked back home around the lake past the edge of the Aleut village.

Crossing the lake from near the log house to where an upper lake [Tanignak Lake] emptied into the lower one [Icehouse Lake or Mirror Lake] were the remains of many piling sticking above the water. The early Russians had a tramway across the "Lower Lake," as it was called then, to transport the wheat to their gristmill, which was located with a sawmill at this point [near the outlet of the upper lake]. The old windlass, powered by a waterwheel, and the sawdust pile were still there. So were some of the burrs that were used to grind flour.

One of the first things I wondered about at Wood Island was why spruce stumps stuck up three feet above the water all over the upper lake. I had never seen trees that grew up through a lake before. It took me a while to figure it out, but of course it is now as plain as day.

First, this "Upper Lake," as it was called, wasn't a lake at all to start with. However, there were at least two more lakes higher up on the island, each of which emptied into the next lower one by a creek that connected this string of lakes. What was now Upper Lake was originally a wide, wooded valley through which the creek flowed. The valley narrowed just above where the creek emptied into the Lower Lake, and the early Russians had built an earthen dam across this narrow outlet and flooded the valley with water.

When this lake had frozen, they cut down the trees at about waist height and made sawlogs of the lower portions and pilings from the upper. When the snow and ice had melted, they floated the logs to the sawmill, where they were pulled into the mill by the windlass and sawed into lumber by power from the waterwheel. [Water to drive the wheel had to come from the two or more higher lakes, which must have been man-made also, as there is no longer any clear evidence of their locations or of the delivery system.]

The pilings were floated to the dam, pulled and pushed over, and floated to their proper locations where they were driven into the lake bottom to support the tramway. The caps, stringers, and planking for the tramway came from the mill.

Mr. Pavloff said the wheat was raised in the Russian River Valley in California and transported in Russian schooners to Wood Island to be ground. What flour they needed for their own consumption was kept there, as was the amount they needed to trade with natives for furs all over Alaska. The balance was shipped back on the schooners' return trips and disposed of at trading posts all the way to California.

Pavloff also told us that large bells, some as large as the Liberty Bell, were cast at Kodiak in much earlier times, and those that weren't sold in Alaska were taken south by these schooners and traded to the early Franciscan Missions in California.

[Surprisingly the author did not mention the ingenious

"business" of the San Francisco-based ice company that was moved from Sitka to Wood Island in 1857. Blocks of ice cut from Tanignak Lake were stored in buildings on the spit between Icehouse (Mirror) Lake and the strait, awaiting shipment to San Francisco. Evidently the author failed to connect the mill and its sawdust and the tramway with the movement, packing, and storage of ice, although Pavloff surely would have talked about the ice business in his presence. As described by Eli Lundy Huggins (*Kodiak and Afognak Life, 1868—1870,* The Limestone Press, 1981, pp. 21-23), the actual shipment of ice to San Francisco was continued into the 1870s. The state of decay of the facilities in 1893 indicates how rapidly they must have deteriorated once maintenance was discontinued.]

Swimming and Boating

During the long summer days the lake got warm enough to make swimming enjoyable. A new clerk and bookkeeper arrived for the North American Commercial Company. His name was Marsden. He soon attracted attention by his expert swimming. He knew the strokes, the Australian crawl and the others. He would go to the Lower Lake in his bathing clothes and swim back and forth, lengthwise and crosswise. We all enjoyed watching him swim. We saw how much fun he was having, and the children, including Aleut children, were now going swimming and learning how to swim.

Very few of the older Aleuts could swim a stroke. Yet out in the strait from the wharf, on several occasions, I can remember seeing Aleuts practicing seamanship in their bidarkas, wearing skin coats with puckering strings around their necks and the hatches to keep the water out. These men were practicing rolling over and righting their bidarkas. They would capsize their boats and come up out of the water on the other side by using their paddles. Yet these men had never learned to swim.

The Greenfield Party

The Greenfields had two milk cows, and with the superabundance of grass on the island, the cows had reached their peak of milk production. Mrs. Greenfield said every pan and pitcher she had was full of rich milk and cream. The cows gave so much milk, she would skim off the cream and feed the skimmed milk to the two hogs she was fattening with slops from her kitchen, plus a little grain.

One day Mrs. Greenfield came to visit Mother. She brought a large cream cake with plenty of whipped cream between the layers and over the top. She said she was trying out a new recipe, and instead of making one cake, she had made two, one for the Greenfields and one for the Roscoes.

By this time, Mother and Mrs. Greenfield had become close friends. Mrs. Greenfield said to Mother, "Ida, next Saturday we're going to have a get-together at our house. The Washburns, the Blodgetts, the Caldwells, and some others from Kodiak are coming over. In all, there will be a couple of boatloads. Could you come early and help get things ready?"

The personnel from the Alaska Commercial Company and the North American Commercial Company were rivals in buying furs and selling goods and trying to get their schooners to the different stations first for these purposes. But every now and then, one or the other would give a party and invite the others, and all their trade rivalry was forgotten, and they always had a wonderful time.

This get-together was no exception. They had games for the children and adults, refreshments, and above all, a lot of friendly talk and gossip. When the party was over, we all walked down to the wharf with the people from Kodiak to see them off in their boats and bid them goodnight. By then I was almost eight, and all these folks were old friends of mine.

CHAPTER 12

THE MISSION

Kadiak Orphanage, 1893.

Across the Lake

By this time the framework of the Mission was pretty well up on the east half. Father put the carpenters to work enclosing rooms and laying the roof on this part so we could move in before the rest of the building was finished.

The stove was set up in the kitchen, and temporary tables were made for the kitchen, dining room, and living quarters. Benches were made for the dinner table and living quarters, where a large box-type heating stove was set up.

The cooking utensils and groceries were moved over first, and Mother began getting the noonday meal ready. During the afternoon the rest of our belongings were moved, the beds were set up and made, and most things were arranged where they were supposed to be.

Mother continued cooking for everybody who came to eat, and as soon as enough additional bedrooms were enclosed, the carpenters' beds and baggage were moved over from the log house and the schooner.

Ofdotia Returns

I went to Kodiak with Father. We tied the boat to the wharf and went up to the store. Captain Charles Brown came in while we were there. He and Father had been close friends ever since Father and Crit Tolman had sailed with Captain Brown on one of their early bear hunting trips to Afognak Island. Captain Brown said his daughter Ofdotia wanted to come and live at the Mission. Father told him he would get a room ready for Ofdotia as soon as he could.

Ofdotia had stayed with us a lot when we were at Kodiak. Her mother, who was part Russian and part native, had died when she was a small girl. Ofdotia had gone to Father's school, and Mother had taught her how to sew and make her own clothes. She had always been a remarkable girl, responsible and trustworthy in every way. She would be a great help to Mother, and I was delighted at the prospect of having her with us again.

A few days later, Father sent word to Mrs. Washburn that a room at the Mission was now ready for Ofdotia. Captain Hanson had just arrived in St. Paul Harbor with his schooner *Kodiak* and, as usual, would be in port for a few days. The steamer *St. Paul* had also arrived in Kodiak from Seattle [with Capt. E. C. Erskine as Master].

Captain Hanson and Mrs. Washburn, with two ladies from Seattle who were taking an excursion on the *St. Paul,* sailed across the strait in a sea otter boat to visit Father and Mother and see the Mission construction.

My folks were always happy to welcome interested strangers along with old friends from our Kodiak days, and Father invariably invited them to stay for dinner before returning. This occasion was special, however, because Mrs. Washburn had brought Ofdotia with them as a surprise.

Of course we were all delighted to see her again, and she was equally happy to be with us. From that day on, Ofdotia took an intense interest in the development of the Mission and quickly became Mother's right hand in caring for the other children as they began arriving from all over the Aleutian area. No more dependable person ever lived than Ofdotia Brown.

The Devil's Brew

It was after midnight when there came a big knock on the door and a woman's voice calling as if she were in pain.

Father got up and went to the door, and there was Mushwa, an Aleut squaw who had a Scotch sailor for a husband. Mushwa was crying and had blood all over her face. Her eyes were blacked and nearly swollen shut. She was "beat up" all over.

She sobbed, "Scotty, drink peeva, go wild."

He had knocked out three Aleuts with a club and had then turned on Mushwa. She said she got away and outran him, and she wanted to stay at the Mission all night because there was no place else where she would be safe. She said Scotty would kill her if he found her.

It was obvious the poor thing was in danger and in awful shape.

Mother built a fire and heated water. She washed the blood off Mushwa's face and body and then gave her a warm bath and clean night clothes to sleep in.

The next day Mushwa was so sore she could hardly get around. She stayed three nights and then wanted to go home. She said the peeva would be all drunk up by then, and Scotty would be sober.

Mother made her a present of the night clothes, and Mushwa went home as if nothing had happened, except she was still pretty lame.

Pavloff's Friendship

Mr. Pavloff came to the Mission to bring us some vegetables from his remarkable garden. He brought rhubarb for pies, lettuce and radishes for salads, turnips for stews, and other vegetables I don't remember.

He stayed for a long visit with Mother and Father while looking over the Mission. He had a very large family and was especially interested in the room that was being built for the classroom and also for Sunday school.

As I have said, he was always sympathetic with the work the folks were doing—in striking contrast with the attitude taken by the majority of the Russian priests.

Pavloff said, "Ida and Ernest, if this school and Sunday school will do as much for my clildren as the Americans did for me at Russian River, I will be very grateful."

Ditto the Bowens

The Bowens lived three-quarters of a mile or more up by the lake near the sawdust pile where the early Russians had the sawmill. Captain Bowen was at the Company store a good share of the time when he wasn't away on a schooner on a fur buying and trading expedition. Soon after Mr. Pavloff's visit, the Captain had taken the afternoon off, and he and his wife and part of their family came walking down the Mission side of the lake to visit us and see what progress was being made.

Mrs. Bowen was the Russian woman who showed Mother how to make those wonderful fish pies the Russians called "perog," and the Bowens were anxious for the schoolroom to be finished so they, too, could send their children to school. The older children, Rufus, Ollie, and David, had gone to Father's school when we were in Kodiak. Once the Mission was finished, the Bowens often came to visit us in the evenings, as both families had done in Kodiak.

Ezekiel

A new man came to help at the North American Commercial Company's office and to buy furs and sell merchandise in the store. He was a Mr. Ezekiel, and he had previously been a successful fur trader all over the northern country. He had traveled and traded up the Yukon and along the main rivers and trails all the way to the Arctic past Point Barrow.

It seems he had decided he had done enough traveling and had come to Wood Island as a permanent fixture. Ezekiel came over to the Mission to see Father and said that he wanted to send for his family in San Francisco, provided his children could attend the Mission school.

Father explained that the school was open for any children who wished to attend, that the Mission was running the school the same as any public school, and that Dr. Sheldon Jackson had promised that the United States Government would take it over as soon as funds could be appropriated.

Ezekiel sent for his family. In a short time the family arrived and moved into a large two-story house that had just been built by the Company at the head of the lake. It was a short distance from Captain Bowen's house.

Accompanying the Ezekiel family was Mrs. Ezekiel's brother,

Elick Stewart. Elick helped around the house, doing the washing, chopping wood, and other chores, and he also did odd jobs around the island whenever they turned up.

As soon as the Ezekiels were settled in their new home, the children started attending school. There were two boys, Edgar and Willie, and three girls, Clara, Frances, and Eve, and they were all very bright students and a joy to Mother and Ofdotia.

Ezekiel soon proved his reputation as a fur trader was well justified. It was the usual thing to see him doing a lot of business at the store, fitting out trappers, hunters, and other traders, and buying furs as they were brought to the store to sell.

Mr. and Mrs. Ezekiel often came to visit Mother and Father at the Mission. They were wonderful neighbors and most grateful for having such a good school for their children.

The Ezekiels also became great friends of the Greenfields, Bowens, and Pavloffs, and one evening all of the adults went over to the Ezekiels' house and gave them a surprise party, complete with cream cakes, cranberry pies, and other refreshments. It was then that they learned many details about Ezekiel's trading expeditions in the far north and all over the vast Alaska territory.

The Death of Arcintee

Johnnie Ponfillof, Nicoli Yerocollif, and the Sargent boys came to see Mother and Father again, as they had promised. Antone Dimedof was on a trading expedition and couldn't come this time. It was a beautiful day, and of course Father invited them all to stay for dinner and Sunday school.

It was clear they had something they wanted to tell Mother, and finally it came out that Arcintee had died a few days before our return to Alaska. We already knew Arcintee was no longer at Kodiak, but no one had told us he had died.

Eddie told Mother that Arcintee knew we were on our way on the *Kodiak*, and while having dinner at the Sargents' house, he had asked Eddie to tell his mother (meaning my mother),

"Want to see White Mama once more. I die pretty soon, not see her." He missed seeing her by only a few days.

Then it came out that the boys had intended to tell Mother about Arcintee's death and what he had said on their first visit but had been unable to do so, and that was what they were thinking about when they seemed troubled as they were leaving and promised to come back soon.

Miss Carrie C. Currant

At about the same time in that summer of 1893, Miss Carrie C. Currant, who had been active in the Woman's Home Mission Society in Boston, came to Wood Island to teach the school that father was about to start in the new Baptist Home Mission and to help with the missionary work. She was a remarkable young woman, an excellent teacher, and the children and adults all thought the world of her.

Miss Currant was often seen with a number of children back in the woods and in the open country gathering flowers, of which there was a great variety. She often went berrying with them when berries were ripe. The children were fond of having her read stories to them, and she was good help with the other work at the Mission.

A Salvage Job

A trading schooner anchored in the strait. The Captain and First Mate knew Mother and Father from our Kodiak days. They rowed ashore and came directly to the Mission.

The Captain said, "Ida and Ernest, we have brought you two boys from Sand Point. They haven't any home and have just been running from pillar to post wherever they could stay, often in the worst company possible. These are boys you can really help in your institution. Are you prepared to take them in now?"

Father answered, "Yes, we are prepared. We have enough

rooms now, so we can take them. Ida and I want to thank you for your kindness to these poor children. If we all work together, we should accomplish much that we can be thankful for in the years to come."

Father went back across the lake in the boat with the Captain and Mate. The Captain took a looking glass out of his pocket and flashed a signal to the schooner. They could see a boat being lowered, and a couple of seamen rowed ashore with the two boys.

As they were coming ashore, Father invited the Captain and Mate to stay for dinner with the boys at the Mission and get acquainted with the plans he and Mother were trying to put into effect for the future of the orphanage.

Robert and Swipes

The Captain introduced the boys when they got ashore. One was Robert, and the other was called "Swipes," a moniker he earned for stealing food to eat from the store at Sand Point, the Captain said.

They all came back across the lake in the dory and walked the last hundred yards up to the Mission. The boys seemed delighted with their new home. They immediately began calling Father and Mother "Papa" and "Mama." Evidently they had already learned a lot about how to get along in this world.

After the Captain and Mate had left, Mother started to clean up the boys. She gave them both baths and new clothes. She cut Swipes' hair with scissors and clippers and applied a solution on his head to kill the lice and nits.

Robert didn't have much hair. His head was covered with sores. Mother fixed him up the best she could by putting iodine on the sores and pasting a white cloth over the top of his head to keep the lice off. She changed the cloth daily and doctored him until the sores were healed. Soon the hair started growing back all over his head.

By now they were different looking boys from the ones who had come off the ship from Sand Point. Still, Mother worried because Swipes wasn't eating as much as she thought he should.

"Swipes," she said, "why don't you eat more? You eat hardly anything."

Swipes replied, "Mama, don't you know that when you haven't had much to eat for a long time and you eat a big meal, it makes you awful sick?"

Swipes' appetite soon improved.

Kitty Feeny

Captain Feeny, the man who had raised foxes since the early eighties on the next island a short distance from Wood Island, had a daughter Kitty by his native wife. The Captain brought Kitty to live at the Mission.

Kitty was a bright and beautiful little girl. The Mission could do much for her, and Kitty liked very much living there. She became fond of Mother right from the start and soon lost her shyness. As other children came to live at the Mission, Kitty became the center of much attention and was a happy child in this nourishing environment.

Miss Currant's Report

Soon after her arrival at the Mission, Miss Currant had written this letter to Mrs. James McWhinnie of the Woman's American Baptist Home Mission Society in Boston, Massachusetts:

> Wood Island, Kodiak, Alaska, July 20, 1893.
>
> My Dear Mrs. McWhinnie:——You will see by the heading of this letter that at last I have arrived here and safely, on the last steamer, but oh, so sick for five days [across the Gulf of Alaska]. The trip on the *Queen* [up the inland passage] was very pleasant but very cold. I got

here on Wednesday morning, July 19th. Mr. and Mrs. Roscoe met me at the beach. I had to come off the steamer on a row boat, then cross a narrow strip of land, and cross the lake in front of the Mission.

The home looked very pretty from the steamer as we came up the bay. The house is getting along nicely. We are in it, that is, we are living in three of the rooms. We have five children now, and more coming very soon. We find we have our hands full with these. If they continue to come, as they have, you will have to be looking for another missionary.

Will you tell Miss Stedman those scissors she gave me have already been put to use, for this morning Mrs. Roscoe shaved every head, and I took them and washed them, for there was great need of it. You ought to see some of the clothes we took off of them. I wish you could have sat here and just seen them as we put clean clothes on them, it would have gone to your heart as it did to mine. They never saw such things before. After we had dressed them up, one little girl went away by herself. I followed her. She had gone around the corner of the house and was looking at herself and her clothes. She looked up in my face and smiled so pleased and happy. I wanted to speak to her but she could not understand English.

The Greek priest here is doing what he can to oppose. Pray God that he may not harm us [between 1889 and 1893, the senior priest at Kodiak was Alexander Martysh; sometime during 1893 he was succeeded by Tikhon Shelamov; in 1896 Martysh was the senior priest at Afognak].

We have four carpenters at work, and the work is going on nicely. It is very cold now, and Mrs. Roscoe says it will be very cold in the winter. The island is just beautiful now, and I have gathered so many wild flowers, and the trees in the woods just hang with moss. It looks like a Florida forest, but the season is so short it ought to be lovely.

I find Mr. and Mrs. Roscoe very pleasant people. She is so good to the children; she treats them like her own. Mr. Roscoe has a little garden planted, and things will grow nicely, although the soil is black sand.

I had a pleasant voyage, I went up on top of the Muir Glacier. I visited all of the missions on the way. The first place we stopped at was Ft. Wrangle, and there I got my first glimpse of the people here, and I was just about heartbroken. I left the company and went to my stateroom and thanked God that He had let me come to this people, for they did look so wretched; it did not make me homesick.

I wish you could have been here last evening when we gathered the little ones around us for prayers. How I did thank God, for the Society work, and for your ladies putting this Mission here. We expect to have the diningroom and dormitory ready this week. The food is so different here, canned goods almost entirely.

We know you all have been praying for us, we have felt it. Do continue to, and God will certainly bless this work.

Yours in Christ,

C. C. Currant

Dr. Jackson

The U. S. revenue cutter *Bear* [mastered by the Irish-Negro Capt. Mike Healy] had cast anchor in the strait southeast of St. Paul Harbor. Dr. Sheldon Jackson was aboard. He came over to Wood Island from Kodiak to see how the Mission building was progressing and to visit the folks and get whatever information might be helpful in his missionary and education work.

He was going as far north as Point Barrow, and the *Bear* was loaded with lumber to build additional Presbyterian schools and churches. On his way back he planned to take a trip up the Yukon while the *Bear* was off on some local missions. He would be picked up by the *Bear* later and would see the folks again on the cutter's return to Kodiak.

When the *Bear* returned to Kodiak, Dr. Jackson had much to say about his plan of importing Asiatic reindeer to increase

the Alaska natives' meat supply. He said there were millions
of acres of the finest kind of reindeer moss growing in the
territory, and what was lacking was reindeer to eat this moss.
He said he was going to try to get an appropriation for this
purpose the next time Congress met in Washington, D. C.

It was hard to get him to talk about anything else, but
Father was persistent and told Rev. Jackson how badly he
needed a government-paid teacher for the school to reduce the
demands on Father and Mother and Miss Currant and let them
give more attention to the Mission children and improving the
plight of the natives.

Dr. Jackson assured Father that the government would
send a salaried teacher to Wood Island as soon as Congress
appropriated sufficient money. This promise was redeemed
after Mother and Father had left Wood Island and returned to
the States.

The *Bear* with Dr. Jackson aboard cast off for San Francisco, and from there he proceeded directly to Washington
where he wrote the following letter to Mrs. McWhinnie:

Washington, D. C., Oct. 9, 1893

Mrs. James McWhinnie, Sup't of Alaska Work

My Dear Madam:—— I spent a day at Wood Island
with Mr. and Mrs. Roscoe and Miss Currant, and enjoyed
it very much. The building was nearly completed. They
were finishing off the upstairs portion. Four carpenters
were still at work and they were making rapid progress.
I found five children in the Home, besides Mr. Roscoe's
family. I called at Karluk on my way to Wood Island and
tried to influence the leading white men to get children
for the Home, but found that the Greek priest had spent
his summer in going from settlement to settlement and
forbidding the people sending children or allowing any
children to go to the Home [evidently the priest in
question was Alexander Martysh who was succeeded by

Tikhon Shelamov in the Kodiak church at about this time]. And in order to help keep children from the Home, he had promised to build a home at Kadiak and take their orphan children. The building, however, that he is erecting is a log building, not very large. The logs were laid up to the height of the walls (to the eaves), and I suspect they will remain in that condition all winter. I do not think that he will be able to open his Home at all until next spring, and when he does, there will be very little room for children. The success in getting children at the Methodist mission at Unalaska, notwithstanding the opposition of the Greek church, has been so good that I am more hopeful of the number that Mr. Roscoe will be able to get at Wood Island. . . .Rejoicing at the good substantial building that the ladies have erected and the beautiful location that has been selected, I remain,

Very respectfully yours,

Sheldon Jackson

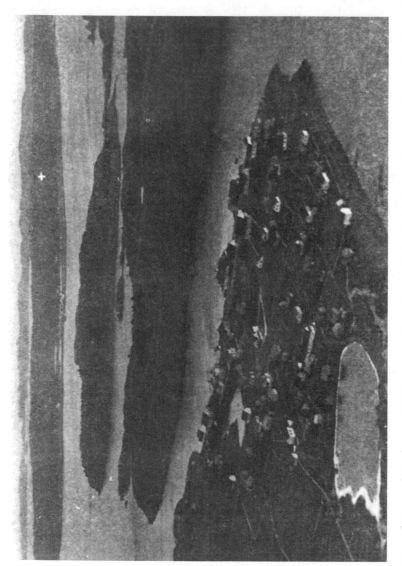

Kodiak village and St. Paul Harbor in 1888, showing locations of Islands to the east in ascending order: Near, Holliday, Wood, and Long. Cross shows location of future Baptist Mission.

A view of the Kodiak Baptist Mission complex on Wood Island taken about 1910, showing the Winch dormitory (left), the chapel built in 1896, and the original orphanage headquarters all reflected from Mirror Lake (photo courtesy of Ella Chabitnoy, who lived in the Mission as a child, via Yule Chaffin).

A later picture of the Baptist Mission complex on Wood Island, taken from the top of the wireless station tower and showing the Winch dormatory (left), the chapel, a good view of the garden, the chicken house, and the original orphanage. Lake Tanignak is just out of sight to the left. (photo by Margaret Learn Ferris, courtesy of Yule Chaffin)

CHAPTER 13

BOUNTIFUL HARVEST

Blueberries

Earlier in the summer, Swipes and Robert and I had found
a good Nova Scotia blueberry patch a mile and a half or so from
the Mission. When we told Mother, she was delighted and
immediately made plans to go berrying as soon as she could
find time.

All her life, Mother loved to pick berries. In a day or two
she could stand the Mission routine no longer, and we struck
out for the berry patch. It was certainly worth the hike for
Mother, because the bushes grew from 18 inches to two feet
high, and they were loaded with large blueberries. Each of us
had a water bucket, and we filled all four and walked back to
the Mission.

The next evening, each of the children and adults had a
large piece of blueberry pie for dessert after supper. Mother
kept some berries fresh for more pies during the next few days
and canned the rest in jars for future pies during the winter.

But Mother couldn't stand the thought of all those other
berries out there on the bushes that would go to waste, so back
out we went several times over the next few days, and Mother
canned those berries too. It would be a wonderful winter.

But in the meantime, there were the red and yellow
salmonberries to attend to much closer to the Mission. Because they would turn to a watery soup if not eaten soon after
they were picked, we would pick them just before a meal.
Mother would time the baking of the shortcake just right to
slap the freshly picked berries into it, and we would all eat the
hot cake as soon as it came out of the oven and was loaded with
salmonberries. The salmonberry shortcakes were delicious
when this procedure was followed.

Loleta

One day Mrs. Greenfield came over to the Mission and said
to Mother, "Ida, both my cows have calves, and I am getting
more milk than I can use. You need a cow now, with all these

children and others who will come. I will sell you Loleta for $60."

Now, as Mother knew, this Loleta was a fine Durham milk cow, and it would be hard to pick out a better one anyplace. So Mother was more than pleased to have the opportunity. She accepted at once and thanked Mrs. Greenfield for making the generous offer.

Father had two of the carpenters get busy constructing a cow barn. It was soon finished, and Loleta was led over to her new home where she was milked. Then she was turned out to eat grass on the Mission side of the lake.

It was Swipes and Robert's job to bring Loleta into the barn to be milked, and when they were bringing her in, we could see them stop along the way and take turns milking her into the other's mouth. They loved the warm, fresh milk, and after Loleta was milked they had all they wanted to drink.

The grass was wonderful, and Loleta gave a bucket and a half at each milking, three times a day. Swipes said, "Why don't you milk her oftener? You would get lots of milk."

First U. S. Judge

Soon after we returned to Alaska, Kodiak had its first United States judge, a Judge Edwards, and also a U. S. marshal. The first marshal appointed during the "Judge Edwards reign" was a young man named Lane, who was well thought of by everyone. Unfortunately, he soon got sick and died.

The marshal who replaced Lane didn't prove to be so popular. Soon he and Judge Edwards became the main topics of conversation around Kodiak and Wood Island. It seemed to me, from the conversations I heard, that the marshal was making a practice of watching for men off vessels and others who looked like easy prey.

When he saw a sailor, for instance, with a flour sack of laundry he was bringing from a native woman's house, or any place else the marshal thought "suspicious," he would grab the sack and search it.

If the marshal found any peeva or other liquor in the sack, he would arrest the sailor and take him before Judge Edwards, where he would be searched for money and usually fined whatever amount he had on him before being allowed to go back to his vessel—a lucrative practice for both the judge and the marshal which continued for some time, as you will see.

Swipes Swears Off

One day Swipes and Robert and I went through the village on our way to the beach. Some of the squaws and papooses were eating. The squaws were dipping pieces of bread in the whale oil in a big, white bed chamber on the center of the table, as was in vogue in those days, and alternately feeding themselves and the papooses.

Swipes liked whale oil, he said, and tried eating a piece of bread dipped in oil that one of the women offered him. It made him sick at his stomach, and he gagged and lay on the ground and vomited for some little time. He said he would never try to eat whale oil again.

Making Hay

The meadow on the south side of the island that Father had included in the land survey now belonged to the Mission. It had tall, delicious grass ready to be cut for hay. Father bought scythes at the store, and he and the boys cut the grass to be cured for Loleta's winter feed. As it happened, the weather was ideal for curing hay, warm sunshine and enough wind to hurry the drying. Before long the hay was ready to be put up.

Father understood the binding of hay by hand, and this knowledge came in handy, as this was before the advent of self-binders. He showed the boys how to bind the hay and carry the bundles to the edge of the field and throw them over the cliff. On the beach they loaded the bundles into the boat and transported them around the point to as near as they could get to the barn. There were no horses on the island yet, and the hay had to be carried by hand from the boat to the barn, a hard way to move hay.

Father was not the only one making hay that summer. The Company also needed hay for their stock, and they had a liter nearby that they loaded with hay from another meadow and towed around to their landing. Mr. Pavloff was also working at a meadow a short distance from where Father and the boys were. Pavloff had some young natives helping him put up his winter's hay. All brought lunches, and when noon came a fire would be lighted and coffee made for all. It was like a picnic.

Fish Pie

One day Mr. Pavloff brought along a young Aleut who appeared to be 21 or 22. Pavloff said to Father, "Ernest, here is a boy who would like a job helping you with the hay. I know him well, and he is an exceptional worker. You will like him."

Father hired the young man, and he was everything Pavloff had said, and more. He and Father kept going out in the boat and getting loads of cured hay, then carrying the hay from the boat to the barn until they had enough stored for the winter.

There was nothing that most of the natives liked better than white man's food, unless it was peeva or whiskey. But, believe it or not, this native boy wouldn't drink either one. Why, we never knew, but we were told by those who should know that when the others were drinking and someone offered him a drink, he would say, "No want 'em." He absolutely refused to drink alcohol.

Mother made one of those big fish pies that Mrs. Bowen had taught her to make, using a whole salmon as usual. The boy came to the Mission when he and Father had finished storing the last boatload of hay, and Mother fixed a meal for him. He must have liked the perog and everything else on the table, for he ate and ate until the whole pie was gone and most of the other food.

The young man didn't seem to have a name. When asked what his name was, he would reply, "No got," and that was all the answer you could get from him. Some of the carpenters started calling him "the fish pie boy," and the name "Fish Pie" stuck to him from then on.

After all the hay was in the barn, Father kept Fish Pie working cutting spruce poles and trimming them for a garden fence down by the lake. Thereafter, whenever someone else wanted a job done well and fast, word would be sent by one of the natives, and Fish Pie was always ready to work if he were not already doing some job for Father.

The Humboldt Washer

Mother's responsibilities and work were continually increasing as the Mission was nearing completion. Timothy Muldony, a painter working on the building, was also an experienced cook. Father asked Muldony to help Mother in the kitchen while the crew was boarding there. Fortunately, he proved to be a very good cook.

By this time, Ofdotia had taken hold and was doing a lot of the work. She was willing and able to help with the cooking, house cleaning, and clothes washing, which was a big chore in those days, as it was all done by hand, mostly on a washboard.

Father had Mr. Lind build a "Humboldt washer," which was considered good in those days. It was a big wooden barrel mounted on legs, with a paddle mechanism inside that was driven manually by cranking a heavy wooden flywheel. The mechanism caused the paddles to rotate alternately clockwise and counterclockwise, even though the flywheel was turned continuously in one direction.

The paddles were perforated all over with holes so water could pass through but not the clothes. There was a lot of friction as well as a lot of weight, so it took a man or big boy to run it, and it was hard work—too heavy for most women.

Mr. Lind also built a hand-operated wringer with a pair of

rollers spring-loaded against each other and geared to a crank. Wringing out wet clothes was also hard work, but not as hard as cranking the Humboldt washer, so the women generally handled the wringing job.

Katie and Annie

The same schooner that brought Swipes and Robert from Sand Point anchored in the strait again. The Captain and Mate came to the Mission with two little girls, each with a small grip.

Mother answered their knock, and the Captain said, "Ida, we have brought you two nice little girls from Sand Point. Their names are Katie and Annie, Katie and Annie Keene. We know they will be happy and well cared for here with you. We told their mother all about you folks and what you were doing for Alaskan children, and she realized how much better off they would be here than with her."

Father came in from cutting wood and thanked the men again for their helpfulness and kindness—to these children as well as Swipes and Robert— and as usual Father invited them in for dinner, even though it was in the middle of the afternoon. Father made a lot of extra work for Mother, but in all her life she never complained or criticized Father or any other individual, although from time to time she did reveal a low opinion of the general run of old-time, quack doctors.

A Couple of Drunks

The Aleut village at Wood Island had another barrel of peeva ready. Many of the Aleuts and three or four sailors were dead drunk.

Mrs. Greenfield had two hogs running at large between slop feedings. These hogs strolled over to the village, got into the barrel of peeva, and filled up. They started for home but managed to make it only as far as the store. They were squealing, falling down, getting up and trying to walk again, then falling down and squealing some more.

A boat was going to Kodiak, and someone at the store sent word to the marshal to come to Wood Island and take care of a couple of drunks who were lying on the ground outside the store.

The marshal came with two men he had deputized to help him take the drunks to Kodiak. When he saw the "drunks," he flew into a rage, but it seemed there was nothing much he could do about the practical joke.

He went back to Kodiak a very angry man.

Sashka, Lofka, and Mamie

Another schooner came over from another island. It brought an orphan family of three children—Sashka, Lofka, and Mamie. Mother went through the regular procedure, giving them baths, burning their old clothes, cutting their hair, and delousing them.

Sashka had a clubfoot but otherwise seemed normal. Mamie seemed healthy and normal. Poor Lofka, Mother found, had running sores on his legs and arms, deep sores that penetrated to the bone. Mother made swabs and washed out the sores with disinfectant.

There happened to be a better than average Alaska Commercial Company doctor in Kodiak at the time, and Mother sent for him to come and see the boy. The doctor said the sores were from hereditary syphilis. He said it showed up every now and then among the Aleut children as well as the adults, many of whom had it and did not know what it was.

The doctor said Mother should disinfect Lofka's clothing frequently, disinfect and bandage the sores, carefully remove and burn the bandages each day, and then wash her hands well with strong soap. He said that with the better food the boy would be eating, instead of a nearly constant diet of whale oil and fish, Lofka should get much better, but he would always be troubled with the affliction. As precautionary measures, he was to sleep in private quarters and be kept away from other children until the sores had healed.

Pretty good advice for those times.

The Conservationist

Mr. Lind's sailing and carpentering partners had just returned from one of their trading trips. I went over to visit with Mary and Richard Greenfield, and we decided to take a walk down the beach to the lagoon where the schooner was moored.

Richard took his light, single-barrel shotgun and shot a duck and some jacksnipes on the way. We reached the lagoon and from there cut across the island, climbing through spruce timber and salmonberry brush, and came out by a crystal-clear lake covered with yellow water lilies.

Swimming on the lake were a pair of beautiful white swans. Richard said he was going to shoot one, but Mary was outraged and said, "Richard, it would be murder to kill one of those lovely, romantic birds."

Richard didn't want to be thought a murderer by his sister, so he left the swans in peace, and we followed the outlet creek down to the Upper and Lower Lakes. Along the way Richard shot some magpies and some feathers out of an eagle.

When we reached the Upper Lake, we rounded it past Captain Bowen's house, then worked our way down to the Lower Lake and circled the back side to the Greenfield home where Mrs. Greenfield gave me a lot of large razorback clams to take home to Mother for our dinner.

A Namesake

A steamer arrived at Kodiak with mail from the States. Mother got a very nice letter from a Miss Grace Steadman of Boston, Massachusetts. In this letter she said she was contributing to the Home Mission Society enough money to keep one native child at the Wood Island orphanage and would like to have a little native girl given her name.

Just after the letter was received, a girl about eight years old came to the orphanage. Mother gave her the lady's name, and from that time on she was called "Grace Steadman." Grace proved to be a bright girl, and I'm sure Miss Steadman would have been pleased if she could have seen and known her namesake. [The author's memory was faulty in this instance; the name of the Treasurer of the Woman's American Baptist Home Mission Society at that time was Miss Alice E. Stedman.]

The Durham Bull

A North American Commercial Company steamer came to the Wood Island wharf. In addition to groceries, hardware, lumber, dry goods, and other supplies, the cargo included a thoroughbred Durham bull for the Greenfields. This was the first blooded bull brought to Wood Island, so the Greenfields' cows had evidently been bred before they were shipped north, as they had red Durham calves.

The natives' cattle at Wood Island and Kodiak were small and mostly black and white, undoubtedly brought over by the early Russians. These cattle were capable of digging down through the snow with their front feet for moss to eat, the same as reindeer do. They could survive the winter without being fed.

The natives generally put up only enough hay for one or two milk cows. Their annual haystack was very little larger than an ordinary haycock. Once in a while there would be a cow that gave quite a lot of milk, but none of them compared in any way with the fine Durhams and other cattle from the States.

Well, back to the Greenfields' bull. He had a large metal ring in his nose, and to unload him from the steamer, the dock hands tied a rope to this ring and tried to hoist him to the wharf with it. Of course the ring was ripped right out of the flesh of the bull's nose, and those nearby had to take cover, as the bull was understandably mad.

With nobody left on deck to get even with, the bull jumped overboard, swam ashore, and high-tailed it to the woods. The natives were scared of the bull and kept their children close to the village, and the adults were afraid to venture too far from buildings themselves.

The Greenfields expected to see the bull appear again with the cows, but it didn't happen. A couple of the Company's men went looking for the bull. They took their Winchesters along in case they were needed. The men found the bull in the timber near the lake, lying on the ground with a bullet through his neck. It eventually came out that an Aleut hunter had run into the bull at close quarters in the woods. The bull showed fight, and the hunter shot him.

On the next steamer, the Company brought the Greenfields another Durham bull, and this one was brought ashore more sensibly and without incident.

Mushwa's Wedding

After Scotty had recovered from the effects of the earlier peeva party, and Mushwa from the beating Scotty had given her, the schooner on which Scotty sailed set out on another trip to Seattle. When it returned, Scotty got shore leave, and he and Mushwa came to see Father and Mother.

Scotty said, "Ernest, I've had a good payday, and I'm staying sober." He went on to say that he and Mushwa had never had a marriage ceremony, and they wanted Father to marry them.

Mushwa was to have a nice wedding dress, and she wanted Mother to make it for her. Mother explained she had so many duties at the Mission that it would be hard for her to do it. Mother was thinking of Shasha and Tanya, two of the apt pupils she had taught to sew years before at Kodiak, and suggested to Mushwa that she hire one of them to make the dress.

Mushwa's "feathers dropped," in Mother's words, and it was easy to see her disappointment. Mother felt sorry for Mushwa and said, "Mushwa, if you can get one of them to come over, I will cut the material, and she will do the sewing."

This suggestion seemed to please Mushwa very much, and she and Scotty went to Kodiak immediately and hired Shasha to come to Wood Island and make the dress.

While in Kodiak, Mushwa went to the store with Shasha and bought light yellow silk and buttons and braid and other essentials for the dress. The three came back in the boat, and the next day Mother cut out the cloth, and Shasha started sewing the dress on Mother's sewing machine.

When the dress was finally fitted and minor adjustments were made, Mother said, "She is dressed up like a queen."

Mushwa grinned from ear to ear and cried a little.

Mother made a large wedding cake, and the next day Father performed the ceremony with all the Baptist trimmings, as he had done and would do for many others at Kodiak and Wood Island.

CHAPTER 14

THE BAD WITH THE GOOD

La Grippe Revisited

A twin brother of the grippe epidemic that hit Eureka in 1891 found its way to Wood Island in October of 1893. People all over the island, the natives and the rest of us, became deathly sick. Some cases ran into pneumonia. As usual Mother and Father and Mrs. Greenfield were doing all they could to minimize the suffering.

Then the Greenfields came down with the grippe, next the Ezekiels and Bowens, and then the Mission. Within three or four days all were flat on their backs, including Miss Currant and Father and Mother. We were all so sick we could hardly raise our heads.

Mother was as sick as the rest of us, it seemed to me, but she forced herself as she always did and made tea, broth, and other liquids and took them to the bedsides and fed us all. Then she would be flat on her back the same as the rest until she forced herself to do it all over again.

Miss Currant and Fred Haig

Before the grippe epidemic broke out, Miss Currant had been making great progress with the students in the school. Among the many people who visited the school and took an interest in the program was a man named Fred Haig, a fine gentleman as I remember him. Haig was a great bear hunter, trapper, and trader, and he took an immediate interest in Miss Currant and became a frequent visitor at the Mission.

Haig was one of the first to come down with the grippe, but he had a strong constitution and started to get better faster than most. As soon as he could, he came over to the Mission and built fires in all the stoves, chopped more wood as needed, and kept the fires going, including Miss Currant's. None of us who was sick there would ever forget the splendid service rendered by Fred Haig, and I know Miss Currant never did.

After we all got out of our sick beds, it was some time before we began to feel ourselves. Miss Currant must have been as sick

as anyone can be and still survive, and she never recovered fully.
She tried to do her job when the school was opened again after
the awful siege and did all she could to help around the Mission—
in fact more than Mother and Father wanted her to do.

Soon it became apparent that, instead of getting stronger as
the rest of us were, Miss Currant's vitality was gradually waning,
and there were days when she had to stay in her room and rest.
Many times I could see that she had been crying, but she was very
sensitive about telling her troubles to anyone, even Mother.

Mother and Father tried to help by inviting neighbors over for
visits in the evenings, and this seemed to please her considerably.
They all knew, of course, that Miss Currant had been used to
associating continually with her many friends in Boston and that
she missed them in this isolated place.

Dr. Ritz

Dr. Ritz was one of the Alaska Commercial Company's fur
traders, storekeepers, and come-and-go doctors. He had been
away for a while and was back in Kodiak again.

It seems the doctor had been made a deputy U. S. marshal
to help the marshal discharge his duties, or perhaps I should
say, his business. Dr. Ritz, it was claimed, was searching
sailors and others he thought might have peeva in their
laundry sacks—the same as the marshal did.

Many were indignant about being searched without any
warrant, then being brought before Judge Edwards and fined the
amount of money they had on their persons.

One dark night, the doctor went down to the wharf with his
lantern. Some sailors, it was reported, kicked the lantern out of
his hand and gave him the working-over of his life. They walked
all over his body and face and kicked him until he was nearly
dead.

It took him quite a while to recover, but he was no fool and
always maintained he didn't have the least idea who it was that
gave him the beating.

Mr. Hagstrom

More children were gradually being admitted to the Mission. Mother, it seemed, was forever busy delousing and bathing them and burning their old rags and replacing them with new clothes.

Meanwhile, the log house we had occupied before the Mission was ready to move into was now being used by the Company for men off trading vessles and other transients to sleep in while not aboard ships.

A Mr. Hagstrom was staying there and was very sick. He and his brother had been running a salting station, salting salmon, on Kodiak Island several miles from the town of Kodiak. They were finished with the season's salting and had come back to work for the Company at Wood Island.

Mrs. Greenfield came over to the Mission and said to Mother, "Ida, that Mr. Hagstrom seems pretty bad off."

Father and Mother immediately went to see him. He had a high fever. Father went back to the Mission for aconite, and when he returned, Mother gave the man a dose and left instructions with his brother about when and how to administer more doses.

After doing everything she could to make Hagstrom comfortable, Mother told the brother the sick man would be welcome at the Mission and would be taken care of as best we could, if they thought it wise to move him.

The brother thanked Mother but said his brother would rather stay where he was if possible. It was evident he did not want to impose on us any more than necessary. "Ida and Ernest, we never will be able to thank you good people enough," the brother said.

Mother assured him, "We will be over to see your brother from time to time, and don't be afraid to call on us anytime we can do him any good."

For the next several days, Mrs. Greenfield and Mother made hot soups and custards and took them or sent them to Mr. Hagstrom regularly as long as he was sick. My memory tells me he was sick for two or three weeks, and it was a real siege for the poor man.

Care Barrels

A steamer came from San Francisco. In addition to the long-awaited letters and other mail, there were two large barrels of gifts from the same people who had sent us care boxes when we were at Kodiak—the congregation of the First Baptist Church in Eureka and my maternal and paternal grandparents in the Mattole Valley.

The barrel from Eureka contained clothing, toys, books, and candy and nuts for the children and many other items that would come in handy at the Mission. The barrel from our families in the Mattole Valley also held some clothing but mainly dried fruit, corn, and dried venison.

As always, Mother distributed the dried fruit to the Mission children daily until the supply was gone and served dried apple pies and the corn and dried venison at mealtimes. Most of the clothing and all of the toys, candy, and nuts were put away in a closet to await Christmas.

Fencing the Garden

The time was soon coming when snow could be expected, and the lakes would be frozen over. Father had been thinking about next year's garden, and as soon as he found time, he sent word to Fish Pie to come and help him build a fence around the intended patch with the spruce poles and posts Fish Pie had cut and trimmed after the hay was in.

They built the enclosure between the Mission and the lake, just to the right of the trail as you walked toward the lake. Mr. Pavloff assured Father this would be an ideal spot for a garden.

Father and Fish Pie dug the post holes with a spade and set the posts and tamped the dirt in around them until they were solidly embedded. Then they nailed on the poles, and the fence was ready for next year's garden.

Father Plays Cupid

Fred Haig had been away on a trading expedition, and as soon as he returned, Father went over to Kodiak and found Haig in the store and invited him over to the Mission for a visit. Haig and another friend came across the strait for supper, and Father and Mother insisted that they stay all night, which they did.

Both men were exciting story tellers. They told of their trips and experiences on the mainland and other islands, and Miss Currant seemed to be enthralled. The next day she and Haig spent much time together around the Mission. It was evident to all that Miss Currant was in love, and Fred Haig didn't seem to mind the idea himself.

In a short time, Miss Currant was well enough to resume her duties in the Mission schoolroom. Her spirits were higher, and her health seemed better. The school was not only a blessing for the students but also a blessing for Miss Currant during those long intervals without mail from the States, which we all missed.

No Warrant, No Arrest

Gibson with a native put up sail and sailed over to Kodiak in one of their boats from the schooner in the lagoon.

When they returned, Gibson said he was walking down past the Greek Catholic church carrying a bundle when the marshal spied him. The marshal came up to him and said he was going to search the bundle.

Gibson said, "Show me your search warrant, marshal."

The marshal was reaching out to grab the bundle when Gibson pulled a six-shooter and said, "Either produce a search warrant or turn and walk the other way. And keep going, or I'll pull the trigger."

The marshal turned and walked away as he was told.

Gibson went over to Kodiak several times during the next few weeks, but no attempt was ever made to search him again.

Some thought the marshal might swear to a warrant against Gibson for resisting an officer, but it seems nothing was ever heard about the matter from the marshal or the judge.

Christmas Gifts

When the last steamer had come for the season, it brought some boxes from the Woman's American Baptist Home Mission Society in Boston. They contained clothing, toys for the children's Christmas party, and a number of pairs of fine ice skates.

The skates were probably meant as Christmas gifts too, but they would be turned over to the Mission children to use as soon as the lakes froze over sufficiently for safe skating.

Father and Mother also got more enjoyable and practical gifts from Grandfather Roscoe's orchard, a large box of dried apples, another of dried pears, and one of dried silver prunes.

The toys were stored in a closet to await Christmas. The clothing was used as needed, and Mother distributed dried pears and prunes to the children each day as long as they lasted. The dried apples were cooked as needed, and we all enjoyed the applesauce and pies.

The children all said, "This is the best stuff we ever ate."

The Moonlight Perfectionist

The days were getting shorter, and lamps were being burned in the mornings and afternoons. A snowstorm came, and clear, cold weather followed. The lakes froze over several inches thick.

A few of the younger natives had skates they had made themselves. They began skating and having a good time when the sun was above the horizon during the middle of the day.

But everyone was amazed when Marsden, the store clerk, went down to the lake with his skates at night and started skating in the moonlight. It was a magnificent sight to behold, as we had never seen such a truly wonderful skater before. It seemed to us he must have mastered all the maneuvers of a professional skater.

He would have plenty of practice ahead, as there would be all those beautiful, moonlight nights when one could see for miles and miles when the weather was clear. We all went down to the lake to see Marsden's nightly performances when those conditions prevailed.

Father's Frostbite

Something went wrong with the kitchen stove's terra cotta flue. Father put a ladder up against the side of the house and started climbing up to the roof to see what the trouble was and fix it.

Father didn't realize how cold it was and wore only light gloves on his hands. When he was nearly to the top of the ladder, his fingers began to freeze, and he could no longer use his hands to grasp the rungs of the ladder. He suddenly realized what was happening and descended as fast as he safely could without the use of his fingers.

Immediately after reaching the ground, he thrust his hands into the snow to draw the frostbite out. His fingers burned and ached, but the flue had to be fixed.

Shurkie wanted to go up the ladder and fix whatever was wrong, but Father didn't want anyone else injured and insisted on doing it himself. (In later years, men like Father would come to be referred to as "macho.")

Mother warmed a pair of heavier gloves by the heating stove. Father put them on and went up the ladder as fast as he could, found what was plugging the flue and successfully removed it with little difficulty, and came back down in a hurry.

Father sustained no permanent damage from the frostbite, but his hands did bother him for some little time after the incident.

Blizzards and Snow Houses

Every little while we had blizzards that winter of 1893-'94. Snow drifts of various depths could be seen all over the island. Occasionally between blizzards the temperature would rise considerably, and we children would be outside much of the time, making snowmen and snow houses.

Mary and Richard Greenfield and the Bowen and Pavloff children were coming to the Mission to attend school each day during the week, and they often stayed a while after school to play with the Mission children.

We would play until we began to get a little too cold, and then we would crawl into a snow house and stay there until we warmed up some. Then we would crawl back out and play some more. We thought we were having lots of fun.

One-Trial Learning

A spell of comparatively cold, calm weather came at a time when the moon was best for light. Everything looked beautiful at night, and the lakes were covered with clear, smooth ice, the kind that is best to skate on. Many boys were out on the Lower Lake practicing skating, and Marsden was skating all over both the Upper Lake and the Lower Lake.

Waselia Somoshka (translated into English, William Samuel) was also considered a good skater. He was skating from one end of the lake to the other and demonstrating to the other boys how to do this stunt and that on skates. He tried a somersault and hit the back of his head on the ice and cracked his skull.

Waselia was in a coma, and everybody thought he couldn't live, but after two weeks he came to and finally recovered. But he never tried to do another somersault on ice.

Just Too Much

The Mission was running smoothly again when word came from Kodiak that Fred Haig was believed to be drowned. He and a couple of companions had put out to sea in a boat from Cook Inlet and never arrived at Kodiak. A trading schooner found a boat floating upright but nearly full of water, and it was identified as their boat.

Miss Currant was in shock, and her health failed rapidly, to the extent that she felt herself compelled to resign and return to her home in Boston.

Everyone on the island was sick about the tragedy and Miss Currant's grief, and we would all miss her greatly, but neither Mother nor Father nor anyone else questioned her decision to leave.

Almost Christmas

Christmas was very near, and all of us children could hardly stand the excitement. Two or three boat loads of friends would be coming from Kodiak, weather permitting, and preparations were being made for the entertainment and the opening of gifts around the Christmas tree.

Father was spending a lot of time drilling the children on the pieces they would be performing. Ofdotia was reading the words of Christmas carols to the little ones and helping them memorize the tiny pieces they would each speak. Mr. Pavloff came over to lead the singing. He sang several songs with the children and came back every day until they all knew their parts well.

A beautiful spruce tree was cut and erected in the schoolroom. The candles and all decorations were assembled, and Mother and Ofdotia decorated the tree with much merriment.

Mother had the boxes of toys taken to the tree and the names of the Mission children and those who went to school written on the presents. A pile of extras was left under the tree to be distributed to others who came, so that no child would be overlooked.

As at every Christmas party, there would also be presents for the grownups. Both the North American Commercial Company and the Alaska Commercial Company had sent candy and nuts and various other things to be distributed.

Everything was done, and everyone was ready.

Christmas Eve

When the moment arrived, people started coming to the Mission, bringing more presents for one another and placing them under and around the Christmas tree. The boats came from Kodiak, and the local people from the North American Commercial Company started arriving—the Greenfields, the Bowens, the Ezekiels, Marsden, and some others—and the seafaring men from both Kodiak and Wood Island. Mr. Pavloff and his family were there, and the Aleut Chief with his redheaded boy and some other native children.

The program went off splendidly, and everyone remarked how well the children spoke their pieces and praised Mr. Pavloff for the fine job he had done in teaching the singers and leading the singing.

As near as I can figure, there were more than 100 at the Christmas tree celebration. Mr. Greenfield had brought over an old-style box full of apples, much larger than the apple boxes of today. Mr. Lind was Santa Claus and passed out one apple to each one there, and when he had finished there were two apples left in the box.

Winter view of Pyramid Mountain near the eastern coast of Kodiak Island from Lake Louise near the town of Kodiak (photo by George Ameigh, courtesy of Yule Chaffin).

CHAPTER 15

IF WINTER COMES

The Garden by the Lake

The winter passed, and spring broke out. The first thing that Father did after the snow melted and the ground thawed sufficiently was to put in the garden down by the lake. The year before, Mr. Pavloff had shown Father many secrets of gardening on Wood Island, and Pavloff's own garden was a testimonial to his knowledge on the subject.

The ground was spaded the depth of the blade, and every three feet a trench was dug spade deep to allow the ground to drain off the surplus water, caused by snow and ice melting, and to let the sun warm the ground.

Potatoes and several kinds of vegetables were planted in these beds. The beds were fertilized with seaweed and fish. A codfish, flounder, or some other fish was planted by each hill of potatoes. Father put in a large bed of potatoes and got a bumper crop, with about two dozen large Early Rose potatoes in each hill.

From Mr. Pavloff, Father got two or three kinds of rhubarb to plant, and currant and gooseberry shoots and strawberry runners. Everything grew in a remarkably short time with the long days and short nights. Almost immediately, it seemed, there were radishes, and soon thereafter lettuce, celery, onions, peas, turnips, rutabagas, and cabbages.

Father tried an experiment with one bed of potatoes to check on the importance of Pavloff's advice. He planted a wide bed without digging the trenches three feet apart to see how potatoes would do in Alaska using California methods. All the seed potatoes rotted in this bed—not one potato grew—because there was too much water in the ground. In every other bed, planted by Pavloff's method, there was a magnificent stand of potatoes.

The Mission got lots of good from this garden.

The Sanitary Smokehouse

The salmon season was on, and the natives had spruce

poles erected outside their houses with stubs of limbs sticking out about three or four inches. The salmon were hung on these limb stubs to dry in the sun.

When the salmon were ready to eat, a native would reach up and take one off the pole, hit the salmon against the side of the house two or three times (the reason for which will soon be apparent), and take it inside to be eaten.

The Aleut villages had no outhouses. The natives used the outdoors on the back side of each house for a water closet. Of course this unsanitary condition on the back sides of the houses attracted a lot of blowflies, which in turn laid eggs on the fish, and the eggs would soon hatch into maggots.

Mr. Greenfield told the Chief of the Wood Island village he should have a water closet like the white people had, and he gave the Chief some lumber and carpet for that purpose. A large hole was dug, and Fish Pie and the Chief erected a small outhouse over the hole.

All the tribe used the white man's water closet at times, but the Chief needed a smokehouse, so the outhouse was used for both purposes.

"Makes fine smokehouse," declared the Chief.

Greenfield's Advice

Most of the native men were out hunting sea otters. Someone shot a whale in a vital spot, and it came ashore on the opposite side of the island from the Aleut village.

The squaws and larger boys were busy cutting strips of blubber and some of the lean meat and transporting it around the island in their boats. The closest point at which they could beach their boats was about 150 yards from their village.

There was quite a lot of driftwood where they landed, and Mr. Greenfield loaned the Chief a large cast-iron kettle and explained to him that the best way would be to render the whale oil out of the blubber right on the beach where the wood was. They would only have to carry the oil and what meat they wanted to their houses.

The Chief took Greenfield's advice, and the tribe rendered enough oil to last all winter.

Who Killed Finnegan?

A report came to Wood Island that a collector of customs named Finnegan was found submerged in the harbor in front of the Kodiak wharf. Father went over to Kodiak with some others to investigate.

Someone at Kodiak took the men over to a native woman's house where there was evidence of a terrific fight—everything topsy turvy and blood spattered over the walls. They came back over the Brooklyn bridge and found a big pool of blood, where whoever was carrying Finnegan evidently had put him down and rested a while. There were drops of blood here and there all the way to the wharf, where he undoubtedly had been thrown overboard.

Finnegan had the reputation of being mean and ugly and picking fights when drunk, and he was known to have been drinking the last time he was seen alive. Very few people liked him.

There was considerable talk about the affair, and it was investigated to some extent for several days, but the public never learned who had killed Finnegan.

The Coroner's Jury brought in a verdict that Finnegan had met his death by falling off the wharf and hitting his head on a spike sticking out from a piling, thus cutting the top of his scalp off, and then drowning.

Mushwa's Baby

More children were being taken into the Mission right along. Mushwa had a baby several months old and brought the little girl to the Mission for Mother to take care of. My sisters, Agnes and Grace, and the other girls were delighted to have a baby at the Mission, and they were lots of help in taking care of little Angie.

The One That Got Away

A Mr. Winterhaulter came to visit the Greenfields. He loved to hunt and fish and had come to Alaska for that purpose. Winterhaulter came over to the Mission one morning and wanted Father to go fishing with him, and Father let me go along. As usual they took their shotguns to shoot ducks that might fly their way.

The boat was pulled out to the fishing grounds, and the fishing began. We were catching the usual variety of fish, more codfish than anything else, when Winterhaulter hooked something that took off for the open sea. It pulled the boat through the water at a very rapid pace for about 200 yards before the tackle broke. The monster didn't break water, so we had no idea what it was.

We fished some more, and Father and Winterhaulter shot some ducks flying over against the wind. We came home with the ducks and two large washtubs full of fish.

Killing the Devil

The Russian Church was having some kind of a celebration. Many of the natives gathered for the ceremony. Several of the Aleut boys who often visited Mother were at the celebration. Most of the men had guns, and during the celebration they would march around the church three times and then fire the guns.

Mother asked one of the boys what the celebration was about.

He said they were trying to kill the Devil.

Mother asked him what the Devil looked like.

The boy said, "He was small and ran down a hole in the ground when the men were shooting."

The boy had evidently seen a ground squirrel and connected it with what he thought the men were shooting at; hence, the squirrel was the "Devil."

The Dancing Party

A dancing party was given by someone at Wood Island. It seems there was quite a turnout, including some Creole girls who came with a bunch of Japanese sailors. All told, there were two or three boat loads of seafaring men of various nationalities.

When the dance was over, it was said, the Creole girls asked some of the Caucasian sailors if they could ride back to Kodiak with them because they didn't want to return with those "Japs."

The Japanese insisted that the girls go with them, and what started out as an argument soon turned into a free-for-all in which the Japanese were beaten up pretty badly.

When the judge and marshal heard about the affair, the marshal started rounding up the sailors and taking them to the judge, where they were accorded the usual search-and-seizure treatment.

A couple of the sailors who had not yet been located by the marshal came to Father and explained that they were only protecting the girls who had asked for a ride back to Kodiak because they didn't want to ride back "with those Japs."

Father told them they had a right to demand a jury trial. If the judge wouldn't grant it, a complaint would be sent to Sitka.

Judge Edwards didn't refuse the sailors' demand for a jury trial, but he seemed very displeased with Father's advice to them. Nevertheless, it was generally agreed that this encounter slowed down the marshal's and the judge's business activities thereafter.

The Fat of the Land

All the children and adults at the Mission were now enjoying fresh vegetables from the garden by the lake, especially the large, delicious Early Rose potatoes. We had all the fresh milk we could drink from Loleta and fresh eggs from Mother's band of Plymouth Rock chickens, the starters for which she also bought from Mrs. Greenfield. A far cry from the canned food we were eating when we arrived at Wood Island the summer before.

Now another season had rolled around for salmonberry shortcakes and wild cranberry and blueberry pies. And every once in a while, Mother would make one of those huge perogs to go with the wonderful vegetables from Father's garden. Usually she used salmon, but she also used codfish or any other good tasting fish in her perogs.

Father naturally took great pride in his garden, but he gave the Lord the main credit for its success. As the garden came on better and better, his blessings before meals grew longer and longer. They had a standard beginning and a standard ending, but in between Father would hold forth on all manner of benevolences that were currently being bestowed on the Mission.

One evening when Mother had made a perog, Father was in particularly good form. He went on and on about the bountiful harvest, enumerating every item on the table, to say nothing of the warm weather and excellent fishing lately, Mushwa's baby, and all the individual presents sent from the friends and relatives in California months ago for the past Christmas, as well as the presents from the ladies in Boston.

Of course Father's head was bowed, and so were ours, but as time passed and the fish pie was getting cold, we children began peeking up and rolling our eyes at each other. Mother must have noticed what was going on because, although her head was bowed when I looked, I could see she was smiling.

At last I could stand it no longer and jumped up and yelled, "Dad, the house is on fire!"

All the Mission children scrambled out of their chairs and ran out of the room.

When Father determined there was no fire, I was administered the automatic switching for my irreverence, which also seemed to go on and on.

By this time the perog and vegetables were really cold.

A Touching Problem

Mr. Pavloff kept a close eye on the Mission garden and was forever telling Father what a good job he had done, and of course Father would invite him up to the Mission for dinner. Pavloff was always anxious to keep up with the progress since his last visit and to find out how any new children were doing.

On one visit, Mother took Pavloff to see Lofka and explained how much better he was now, since he was cleaned up, his running sores were treated and healed, and he had all the good food he could eat.

Pavloff said, "Ida, I don't see how you can stand to do this. There are very few who would come here and do such work for these poor people."

Then they talked about the unsanitary conditions that existed in the native villages and how important it was to deal with this aspect of the situation in checking the spread of syphilis and other diseases.

The natives used a common dipper or tin cup to drink water from a bucket, with syphlitics and children drinking from the same cup or dipper, and of course there was much bodily contact. The older natives were hard to re-educate, and they were now dying off rapidly, so any strategy for improving the situation had to start with the children, as was being done at the Mission.

Mr. Pavloff said to Mother, "Ida, I thoroughly agree with the approach you and Ernest are taking, and I only wish I could be of more help. I see them all around, at church and elsewhere. I see the syphlitics mingling among and handling the little ones under the most unsanitary conditions. In my position with our church I can do little to help, and I am sorry. I admire your devoted spirit and religion and the sacrifices you are making for these people."

CHAPTER 16

MERRY-GO-ROUND

A Day at the Beach

It was a beautiful day, and everything was happening at once. A revenue cutter was coming into the harbor towing a contraband schooner she had seized. A couple of Company trading schooners were being unloaded at the wharf, and a large school of whales were coming up and spouting all through the strait.

Overhead formations of migrating ducks—mallards, eiders, king eiders, canvasbacks, and many others—could be seen as far as the eye could reach. It was just one of those wonderful Alaska days, and a prettier picture would be hard to visualize.

But the greatest action was occurring along the beach where many native men and boys were wading out into the water and dipping baskets that instantly would be full of small fish.

Millions and millions, no doubt tons and tons, of tiny smelt were spawning in the sand along the beach. The sea gulls and other water fowl were eating as fast as they could. Each small wave would wash silver hake and other predator fish up on the beach. If they weren't immediately picked up by someone, they generally would flop themselves back into the water and continue feasting.

Father, Mother, and all the Mission children went to the beach to witness this remarkable sight. The Greenfields, the Bowens, the Pavloffs, the Ezekiels, and many Aleut women and children were there as well.

Ofdotia carried Ruth, my youngest sister, and was never happier. She thoroughly enjoyed helping Mother with Ruth and with Agnes and Grace, who were playing in the sand on the beach nearby. The Keene girls and Kitty Feeny had their shoes and stockings off and were wading among the fish, reaching down now and then, grabbing a fish and throwing it up in the air, or at one another, and giggling.

Shurkie, Robert, Swipes, and the other boys and I were all over the beach, up to the lake and back and forth, having a lot of fun until time for all to go home to the Mission.

Fortunately, that day was not the end of the fun. The weather continued perfect for several days, and this scene was repeated each day.

Passage to Sitka

In the summer of 1894, Father took passage on the steamer *Bertha* to Sitka to meet with Governor Sheakley concerning missionary work in general and more specifically the petition filed by the senior priest at Kodiak [Tikhon Shelamov] to have Father removed from Wood Island and imprisoned for interfering with the domain of the Russian church.

Joining Father were Mr. Tuck of the Methodist Mission at Unalaska, Mr. Peterson of the Sweedish Mission at Yakutat, and Mr. Shull [or Snell] of the Presbyterian Mission at Sitka. The governor was about to appoint a commission who would formulate new laws for the territory, and Father and the other missionaries met with Mr. Sheakley to state their wishes in regard to the duties of deputy marshals to put orphans in the home missions and enforce compulsory education.

On the way down, the *Bertha* [with Capt. Jacob Hansen as Master] called at all the trading stations of the Alaska Commercial Company. Along the west coast of Prince William Sound, every few minutes they would hear pieces of the gigantic glacier and surrounding terrain break off and wash into the sea. Father said the sound probably could be heard for thirty miles.

At Yakutat they went ashore to trade with the Indians. Father was particularly interested in their status under the teachings of the Swedish missionaries. He had known both Mr. Hendrickson and Mr. Johnston during our earlier stay at Kodiak. They and their lady missionaries, including a Miss Peterson, treated Father royally, and he never forgot their kindness.

As the *Bertha* was approaching Sitka, she got too close to the rocks and scraped off her shoe. Father's prayers expressed his thanks that it was no worse. A little closer and they would have been wrecked.

In Sitka Father saw many old friends. Unfortunately, Dr. Jackson was not there, but Mr. Shull, the superintendent of the splendid Sitka Industrial Training School run by the Presbyterians for the natives, showed Father and a Mr. Tuck through the extensive buildings, from which Father and Tuck gleaned many useful ideas for their own missions.

Mr. Tuck, the Methodist Episcopal missionary from Unalaska, was also aboard the *Bertha* on the return trip. He and Father visited the Indian villages along the way and saw their impressive totem poles and some excellent houses that had been built by young natives who had attended the industrial school in Sitka.

Tuck became interested in Father's account of our Baptist Mission on Wood Island and stopped off at Kodiak to see it and visit with us before prodeeding on to his Mission in the Aleutians.

Father's Impressions

On Father's return from Sitka he reported some impressions of the scenery and living conditions in a letter to Mrs. McWhinnie of the Woman's American Baptist Home Mission Society that appeared in the January 1895 issue of the *Home Mission Echo* under the heading **FROM KADIAK TO SITKA**:

Wood Island, July 21, 1894.

Mrs. James McWhinnie,

Dear Friend:——I promised to write you something about the country from Kadiak to Sitka.

Leaving St. Paul Harbor we sailed Northeast close by Spruce and Marmot Islands, both of the Kadiak group. Marmot Island is uninhabited, except by one or two white men employed to rear black foxes as the island is said to have been leased for this purpose. Crossing the mouth of Cook's Inlet we encountered rather rough water. Soon we sighted the mainland. Passing along these wild, snow-covered, uninhabited mountains, a run of thirty hours from Wood Island brought us to Nuchuck in Prince William Sound. . . .

The wretched Indian women sell their daughters ten or twelve years old, holding them in no higher esteem than mere chattels. White men in this section, as elsewhere, have children by native women. I was told of many orphan children utterly destitute.

We left this beautiful harbor and during the next day and a half we steamed down the coast, passing the settlements of Kyak and Yaketage to Yakutat, situated below Mt. St. Elias. At the base of Mt. St. Elias is a glacier fifty miles long running parallel to the coast. It is of ancient formation; at one end a vast amount of earth has accumulated on which large trees are growing. Its progress down to the sea is very slow. I have never seen anything more grand than Mt. St. Elias, generally said to be the highest mountain of North America. From its rugged, picturesque appearance I should think it would be impossible to climb to its top. The whole range of these Alaskan Alps presents magnificent scenery to the eye of the tourist.

This region is the habitat of a rather peculiar bear known as the St. Elias grizzly. Mountain goats are found high up the mountain sides. An Indian went hunting from Yakutat this year and killed forty bears in less than that many days.

At Yakutat I was surprised by seeing a small collection of well-made houses and a swarm of Indians on the beach, who jumped into their canoes and thronged our vessel. I soon learned . . . that several families usually lived in a house on most amicable terms. On our return Mr. Hendrickson showed Mr. Tuck and myself into such a house. It had one very large room down stairs, several cook stoves, and each family had their own corner, bedstead, etc. At either end of the room stood a large, ancient totem pole. . . .

They have a sawmill, which is a civilizing factor in promoting the building of the large houses instead of the huts that the natives usually live in. About half of the people are nominally members of the Russian Church. All of them seem interested in their spiritual welfare, but hate to give up their heathen customs. They say the Russian religion is an easy religion, since it allows them to dance and get drunk. Now when they get drunk they seem deeply penitent and cry about it. . . .

From Yakutat we were nearly two days getting to Sitka against a head wind. Below Yakutat there was an almost innumerable number of glaciers. As we got near Sitka the mountains became more densely covered with trees. For several hours we steamed through the straits. Once two deer were seen on the beach close to the vessel. The town of Sitka is beautifully situated. The high mountains back of it and the island dotted bay render it one of the most beautiful places on earth. The town contains two sawmills, a custom house, in which are various offices, two hotels, a Presbyterian church, a Russian church, and various good dwelling houses. The Indian settlement is at one end of the town. I visited some of the houses, among the number that of Princess Thom, who was a passenger with us from Yakutat to Sitka. She is a rather noted character, a shrewd trader. She tried to sell me some of their silver trinkets, a silver ring she wanted to sell for $1.50; a bracelet for 75 cents. Another Indian woman (Elizabeth) grabbed my hand and pushed the ring on to my finger thinking to make me buy it.

I learned that the Sitka training school had taught the boys carpentry, and thus they were able now to build these good houses. . . . It was vacation time and the large boys were rafting in logs for wood, salting salmon, etc. . . . The boys make all the shoes for the school and do some shoemaking for other people. They also make the bread. The large girls seemed thoroughly competent in waiting on the table and doing kitchen work. A steam laundry does the washing. . . . The total expense of the school last year was $27,000. . . .

It seems that these Indians all respect one chief or head man. For instance in Sitka . . . they would not obey the U. S. Commissioner and other officials about sending their children to school. Finally the Governor went to their houses and told them to send the children to school, and the school was immediately filled. . . .

Yours in the Master's cause,

W. E. Roscoe

The $5.00 Buck

Somewhere along the way back from Sitka, the Captain of the *Bertha* had bought about 15 buck deer from the natives. Some of the buckmeat was eaten on the way home. The rest was sold when the ship arrived in Kodiak, and Father bought a whole deer for the Mission for $5.00.

Capt. Hansen told Father he made a practice of buying more buckmeat than he needed on any trip and sold what was left over, and Father bought deer from him on several future occasions.

Miss Lulu Goodchild

Miss Carrie Currant had returned to her home in Boston on the last ship out of Kodiak in 1893. As soon as she got off the steamer in San Francisco, she sent her resignation by telegraph to the Woman's American Baptist Home Mission Society, and they very quickly recruited Miss Lulu Goodchild to replace Miss Currant.

However, Miss Goodchild did not actually arrive until the following September [1894], and during that nine-month interval the joint burden of caring for the orphanage and teaching the school children fell entirely on Mother and Father, mainly Mother due to Father's travels and continual difficulties with the priests at Kodiak. As I remember, they each must have worked an average of fifteen hours a day, as did Ofdotia.

We didn't know when a new teacher was coming until

Miss Goodchild arrived at the Mission and introduced herself. Mother asked whether she had eaten, and she replied she had not. So, as always, Mother immediately got busy and soon had a delicious meal for her to eat. I particularly remember her praising Mother's homemade bread.

Boat Trouble

When Mr. Lind had finished the carpenter work on the Mission, he took a steady job with the North American Commercial Company in their carpentry shop. He had borrowed the skiff he had built for the Mission, and it was tied up with many other boats under the Company's wharf. There came an extremely high tide, and several boats broke loose and drifted out to sea with the outgoing tide. Among these was the Mission's skiff.

Father talked with Mr. Greenfield and arranged for Lind to build another skiff for the Mission. While the new boat was being built, Father and Mother borrowed a Company boat to go over to Kodiak. They took me along.

Father and a husky young Aleut were rowing. In making the circle around Near Island next to St. Paul Harbor, they cut in too close to the point and hit a slightly submerged rock. The impact knocked a hole in the boat's bow.

Father and the young Aleut stepped out of the boat and stood on the submerged rock. They tore off a piece of Father's shirt and calked the hole as best they could. Then they got back in the boat and rowed as fast as they could, and Mother and I bailed as fast as we could. We made it around the curve and into the harbor and tied the boat up against the side of the Kodiak wharf.

During the short time we were visiting friends in Kodiak, Yokoff Yerocollif, the master ship carpenter and our old friend and neighbor from earlier times, repaired the boat. Close inspection would be required to see that it had ever been damaged.

Fishing for food

When we returned, I went over to the wharf with some of the boys to fish. We were pulling them out as fast as we could bait our hooks and let them down again, as was usually the case when the weather was right. We caught what we wanted to take home and then kept on fishing for the squaws who had congregated there from the Aleut village.

Most of the men were off hunting. The squaws would carry the fish home as fast as we gave each one a fish. They would say to me in Russian, "Slova mulchiska," meaning "good boy," every time I gave one a fish. Their native diet was principally fish and bread dipped in whale oil.

Exit Judge Edwards

Snow had come again, the lakes had frozen over, and Judge Edwards suddenly had gone totally blind. There was speculation that someone might have given him some bad whiskey, but nobody seemed to know for sure what had happened.

As far as any of us knew, there were no more vessels leaving for the States this season. However, Mr. Greenfield heard of the judge's plight, and notwithstanding his contempt for the way the judge had been running his office, Greenfield was a man of compassion. He sent word to Judge Edwards that the North American Commercial Company was momentarily expecting a steamer to stop at Wood Island briefly on its way out and that the judge could have passage to San Francisco.

The vessel arrived, the blind man was taken aboard, and that was the last we ever heard of Judge Edwards. [However, Judge Edwards did return to Kodiak after the Roscoes had returned to California, and he may have mended his ways somewhat, as implied in the Annual Report of the Woman's American Baptist Home Mission Society for 1896.]

No Somersaults

When those wonderful moonlight nights came once more, with the weather just right and the lakes covered with clear, smooth ice, the young people were again having a wonderful time skating, including the Mission children. Waselia Samoshka had recovered from last year's accident and was exhibiting all kinds of fancy skating to the younger people, with the sole exception of somersaults.

There were several of those perfect moonlight nights that winter.

The Holiday Season

When Christmas came again, there was another spruce tree in the schoolroom with presents and entertainment for all, and Mr. Pavloff led the singing as he had done before.

Mother had saved enough Plymouth Rock roosters for Christmas and New Year's dinners for all. Fish Pie ate Christmas dinner with us. Mother had baked several pans of cookies and had Fish Pie take them to the Aleut village for her when he went home.

The orphanage and school were running smoothly.

CHAPTER 17

IT HAD TO BE DONE

A Terrible Ordeal

Writing from memory, I may be off a little on the exact time, but it must have been shortly after New Year's of 1895 that a Company schooner came to Wood Island with about 20 shipwrecked men. Their schooner had run on a reef off an island several hundred miles distant.

It was impossible, they said, to run a boat ashore on account of the rocks in this reef. The Captain swam ashore in the icy water with a line. It was a considerable distance. He tied the end of the line to a rock so the rest of the men could come ashore on a breeches buoy. Then he froze to death.

Before the men came ashore, they put on all the oil clothing they had over their red flannel underwear and their other clothes. In spite of the oil clothes they got pretty wet from the waves that splashed over them in the breeches buoy. Two or three froze to death on the way into shore.

There was a native village they knew about a few miles away on the other side of the island. The men had to walk around the beach to reach the village because of the rough terrain in the central area. The walk took several hours, and when they arrived, all had fingers or toes or feet or legs frozen.

One man who was luckier than the rest in this respect later explained, "The reason that I'm not worse is that another man who had frozen to death had rubber hip boots. I pulled them off his legs, filled them with salt water, and put them on. I also put his clothes on over mine. I walked to the village, and the boots saved my feet and legs."

The natives had fires to thaw the men out and whale oil for them to eat and did all they could for the men, but as time went on their frozen limbs became worse and worse. Some way the natives got word to the Company schooner, which came to their rescue and brought them to Wood Island.

A Rotten Job

Mr. Greenfield had the sick men moved into the log house

that we had lived in before moving across the lake to the Mission. The house was used as a hospital, and a bed was set up for each man. As this was being done, Greenfield sent a messenger to Kodiak to bring back the current doctor of the Alaska Commercial Company.

The doctor came and, after a quick look, said that mortification of the frozen limbs had set in, and he would have to start amputating. There was a smaller Company log cabin nearby. This was used as the operating room, and one by one the men were taken there for surgery.

The two men who were in the worst shape, Billy Bailey and a Mr. Harman, had to have both legs amputated below the knees. The doctor had very little chloroform, so he filled them up with whiskey, and they had to be strapped to the table and held by four men during the operation.

The doctor operated on Harman first and sawed the first leg off very crooked with a meat saw. It was apparent to Father and the other men helping that the doctor was no mechanic and couldn't saw straight.

Father, who had experience butchering livestock, asked the doctor to let him do the sawing, which the doctor was glad to do.

Father cut away flesh around the bone, leaving flaps of skin and flesh long enough to fit over the end of the stub after the bone had been cut off straight. He pointed the flaps so they could be folded over to fit like the wedges of an orange and sewed together neatly. Then he sawed the bone off and rounded the edges, and the doctor sewed the flaps together.

They did the same with Harman's other leg.

The next day they amputated Billy Bailey's legs, the doctor telling Father how far up to cut and doing only the sewing himself.

For several days after that they were amputating fingers and toes from the various men. One man lost most of his foot. The doctor failed to have the amputations done high enough on several, and the members had to be cut off higher up the next time to get above the mortification.

Friendship and Kindness

Harman and Bailey each had to have his legs amputated three times, the last time nearly to their hips. Harman wasn't getting along as well as Billy, and they moved Harman back to the operating cabin and had him taken care of away from the others.

Harman and Bailey had been friends for many years, and each day Billy would inquire how Harman was doing, and they always told him, "As good as could be expected." After a few weeks, Harman died and was buried.

The next few times Billy asked about Harman, he was told practically the same thing, but Billy sensed that something had changed and said, "You can't fool me any longer. I know Harman is dead."

Billy's stumps finally healed satisfactorily.

During all of this time Mrs. Greenfield and Mother were constantly cooking and taking or sending food over to the log house for the men. Mrs. Ezekiel and Mrs. Bowen also did what they could to make their recoveries a little easier.

In the spring when the snow and ice had melted, Capt. Mike Healy brought the revenue cutter *Bear* to Wood Island to take the men to San Francisco. All the people of the island came to the North American Commercial Company wharf to see them off.

Billy was carried aboard on a stretcher. When he shook hands and bid goodbye to Mother and Mrs. Greenfield, he broke down and cried, saying, "Greater kindness than this I have never seen."

They said, "Goodbye, Billy, God bless you," and I could see tears in their eyes too.

The Big Snow

During the winter of 1894-1895, before the revenue cutter had come to take the amputees to San Francisco, there had been seven months of continual snow all over the island, something very unusual along the path of the Japanese current. Generally the snow would melt earlier than it did that year, and there would be thaws during the winter when much of the ground would show.

When the snow finally melted in the spring of 1895, Father put in his garden once more. By then the days were quite long and the nights short. Father had Robert and Swipes spade around the goosebedrries, rhubarb, currants, and strawberries and rake the beds intb shape. A week later we had wonderful rhubarb pies and soon thereafter radishes, and it wasn't long before the other vegetables were coming to the dinner table.

Gold in Alaska

Mr. Warmburg, another old friend, and a Mr. Erickson came to Kodiak for a few days from their mines on the mainland. They came immediately over to Wood Island to visit Father and Mother and made the Mission their headquarters for most of the time before returning to their mines.

Warmburg and Erickson were enthusiastic about their success since they had got rigged up with better flumes and with giant water nozzles to blast the dirt and rocks into the flumes. They brought a lot of nuggets and flake gold to be shipped out on a steamer from Kodiak.

A little more than a year later, in 1896, more gold was discovered on the Klondike River, and by 1897 the gold rush was on.

The Cannibals

A Company schooner arrived at Wood Island with the remainder of a crew who had survived a shipwreck off an uninhabited island.

Their story was that the whole crew had made it ashore safely, but they were without food, and although they could have caught fish, each was afraid of leaving the others and, while away, being plotted against and killed for food upon returning. The story sounded implausible at first, but apparently more than one had actually met his death that way.

The men stayed pretty much to themselves while waiting for the *Bear* to return and take them away, but a few came into the store now and then.

A clerk asked one of the men how human flesh tasted.

The man replied, "It tastes just like pork, not bad at all when you're hungry."

The Haunted Island

There had been a lot of talk for some time about a "haunted" island between Kodiak and the mainland. Many travelers in these treacherous waters had put into this haven of refuge to get fresh water or, in some cases, for protection from an approaching storm.

A cabin was there and other buildings left by a recluse who had died mysteriously a few years ago. The man was known to have had a large dog, but the dog was nowhere to be found, dead or alive, and this of course added to the mystery.

Most everybody who stopped at the island and stayed overnight reported about the same story.

They would go to bed and soon hear "some of the most damnable noises that one ever heard." They would go outside, and an old grindstone in the yard would be turning at a rapid speed, but nobody would be there. They would go back inside, and there would be loud pounding on the side of the cabin, but when they went outside again, there would still be nobody in sight. If they left any groceries outside, they would invariably disappear, but nobody was ever able to catch the thief.

There was no sign of anybody living in the cabin, and the only things those brave enough to return a second or third time found rearranged or moved could easily have been the work of other seafarers who might have stopped by in the meantime. Some who had stopped there were so alarmed they would never go back if they could possibly avoid it.

What was doing these things nobody knew, but many suspected and some were firmly convinced the island was haunted.

Mr. Cherinoff and Mr. Derinoff, whom we knew well from our Kodiak days, had just arrived at Wood Island and came over to the Mission to visit with Father and Mother. They had a boat load of furs and said they had stopped at the haunted island on their way in.

These free lance fur traders had been there many times before. They said the same things happened to them that were reported by others, but they had discovered fresh tracks of a large dog outside the cabin in the soft dirt after a rain. They had spent considerable time searching for the dog or for any other sign of him or sign of someone living anywhere on the island but were unsuccessful.

Reports of the haunting of the cabin on the island kept coming in, but up to the time we left to return to the States in August of that year, the mystery had not been solved.

The U.S. revenue cutter *Bear* mastered by the Irish-Negro Capt. Mike Haely (photo courtesy of the University of Oregon Library).

CHAPTER 18

THE LAST LAP

Curtis P. Coe

As the summer of 1895 approached, Mother and Father decided it was time to return to California to be close to their families. Mother's mother, my Grandmother Amanda Miner Dudley, had tuberculosis, and although she would live for another ten years, no one knew at that time how long she would last.

The Mission was running smoothly, with about 20 children in the orphanage, as I remember, with Ofdotia the oldest and Angie the youngest. Things were in excellent shape to be turned over to a successor. The Woman's American Baptist Home Mission Society had received Father and Mother's resignation, to be effective at the end of the summer, and a Mr. Curtis P. Coe and his wife had been selected to replace them.

The Coes arrived early in the summer, and Mr. Coe delivered a letter from the Society containing Father's and Mother's salary money for the rest of the summer and instructions to familiarize the Coes with the Mission and introduce them to all the key local people so there would be an orderly transition when the Roscoes left in the fall.

However, it soon became apparent that Mr. Coe intended to take full charge immediately.

Father and Mother talked the situation over, and Father was prepared to assert his authority in accordance with the Society's instructions, but Mother's better judgment and stronger will prevailed, as they always did when she felt the matter really important.

Father made arrangements with Mr. Greenfield for the use of a Company house, and we moved out of the Mission and back across the lake and left the Coes in charge of the orphanage. Father concentrated on getting subscriptions for the construction of the little chapel that would soon be erected after our departure, the first Baptist church in Alaska.

Quick Consumption

During the winter before, my sisters Agnes and Grace had helped Mother a great deal by taking care of Mushwa's baby Angie who was sick most of the time. By then Agnes was seven years old, and Grace was six.

Angie seemed to have recovered from the specific illness, but she wasn't doing well in general, and the folks were worried about her health. She was pale, had very little appetite, and hardly any energy. The poor little thing was a patient baby and almost never cried. We all loved the little one, but I think Agnes and Grace loved her most of all.

Soon after the Coes took over the orphanage, Angie developed the dreaded malady then called "quick consumption." This was the first death at the Mission.

Mushwa wanted Father to conduct the funeral service, but this was not to be. Mr. Coe officiated and gave his first funeral sermon on Wood Island in the Mission schoolroom.

Agnes who was now eight and Grace almost seven were devastated.

The C. P. White

We lived in the borrowed Company house until we got transportation to San Francisco in August. During this time a lot happened.

A capsized schooner was sighted by a North American Commercial Company employee who reported the derelict to Mr. Greenfield. Greenfield sent out the Company's local steamer to tow the capsized schooner to the Wood Island wharf. The vessel was the *C. P. White* from San Francisco.

It seems she was in the Alaska waters poaching on the sea otter that were supposed to be killed only by Alaskan aboriginal natives. However, the *C. P. White* had a completely white crew, hunters and all.

As soon as she was towed to the wharf, operations began to right her again. They fastened empty drums all around her to keep her afloat after the air inside her was lost by turning her back to the upright position.

With the help of a derrick and blocks and tackle on the end of the wharf, the power of the steamer and many natives rolled her over to upright. She was then towed ashore at high tide, and when the tide was out, holes were bored through her bottom and the water drained out.

When they inspected her hold, they found several dead men. The rest had been washed away. The wind was blowing toward Wood Island, and everyone there could testify that there is no more putrid odor than comes from decaying human flesh.

They also found quite a number of fine Parker shotguns, still in salvageable condition, and cartridges loaded with buck shot to shoot the sea otter. One of the Company agents complained that several shotguns disappeared as they were being unloaded.

Wooden plugs were driven in the holes in the hull, and when the tide came in, the *C. P. White* was towed out in the strait and anchored.

The Missing Rug

The dead men had to be buried, and Elick Stewart got the contract for $20 apiece. The rotten bodies were loaded in a sea otter boat and taken across the strait for burial on the first island from Wood Island on the way to Kodiak [Bird Island].

The wind was still blowing in from the strait, and none doubted that Stewart was earning his money on the contract.

The next day Mother noticed that her fine Brussels carpet was missing. The mystery was solved when it came out that her carpet had been used to carry the bodies aboard the sea otter boat, and Stewart thought it best to bury it with them.

During this period the weather had been beautiful, as I have described before, with the straits full of whales, fish, and ducks. If it would only stay this way, what a wonderful place it would be to live.

Decision Time

Father got word that the bark *Harvester* was loading cases of canned salmon at Barlin's cannery at Karluk and we could get passage on her to San Francisco.

The North American Commercial Company's local steamer was about to make a trip around Kodiak Island to the Karluk side, and Mr. Greenfield said this would probably be the only chance for us to get to Karluk before the *Harvester* was scheduled to sail on August 12th. We rushed to get ready during the next two days, and after bidding the Mission children and all our friends an affectionate and tearful farewell, we were on our way home.

Mother had wanted to have Ofdotia come to California with us as a member of our family, but the Coes had come to depend on her to care for the younger children, and Mr. Coe insisted that she stay at the Mission.

Ofdotia loved Mother and wanted to come with us, but she also felt responsible for the children and was willing to stay. She remained at the Mission until 1907 when she moved to Oregon, and years later she told my sister Helen that her life would have been much different and happier if she had come with us to California.

Karluk Interlude

When we arrived at Karluk, most of our baggage was transferred to the *Harvester*. What little personal things we needed were taken ashore in a boat to Mr. Barlin's cannery, which was directly across the Karluk River from the Cutting Packing Company's plant, near the mouth of the river.

Mr. Barlin took us to his house where we would stay for about ten days while waiting for the *Harvester* to be fully loaded. Barlin was a bachelor, and his sister was keeping house for him with the help of a Chinese cook and houseworker. They were fine, hospitable people and immediately made us feel at home with them.

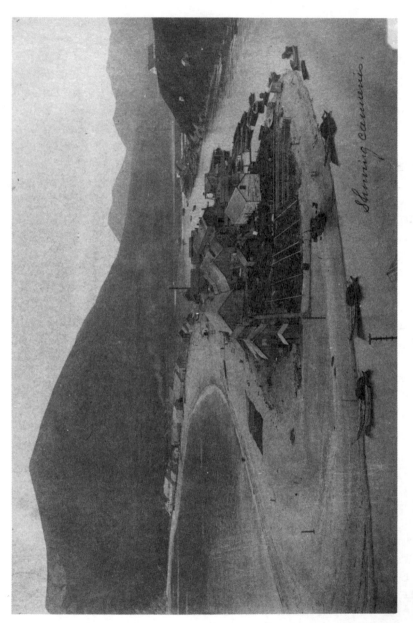

Salmon canneries on the spit at the mouth of the Karluk River on the northwest coast of Kodiak Island in 1897 (photo courtesy of the National Archives).

The Salmon Business

This was an interesting stay for me, with something new continually happening and the weather continuing fine.

I was all around the salmon cannery and observed the whole canning process from where the cans were assembled, the shook made into cases to hold four dozen cans, the cleaning of the salmon, the conveyors taking them up into the cannery, the big vats of salmon cut into proper canning size by one stroke of a big lever operating the knives—the whole process from start to finish.

The workers in the canneries were principally Chinese. They had a cookhouse, but at this cannery during the good weather the Chinese did most of their cooking on the beach. The biggest part of their diet, as I saw it, seemed to be fish, rice, and some bread.

At the mouth of the river, just before the tide turned to come in, the salmon were packed so thick that a man could have walked across the river on their backs—their backs literally stuck out of the water. When the tide turned to come in, the salmon began to move up over the wide, shallow riffle at the head of the estuary. From there, they made their way up this magnificient river to their spawning beds in a beautiful lake at the head of the river where they laid their eggs and died.

While they were waiting in the estuary at the mouth of the river, they were fair game for the fishermen.

The fishermen were white men of various nationalities. On the beach they were seineing the salmon on their side of this wonderful Karluk River. They put out a huge seine from a large, flat-bottomed boat with a long roller on its stern. This barge was towed by a tug. It seems to me the net was about a quarter of a mile long.

After the seine was set out around the salmon, it was pulled as close to the beach as possible by the tug. Ropes were fastened from the net to a large windlass, and several men turned the windlass, winding in the net until the fish were above the water's edge.

Boats then pulled up along the net, and the salmon were

loaded.   The fishermen used one-tined pitchforks, called
"pews," to pitch the salmon into the boats. They got as many
as 30,000 salmon in a single draw of the net.

On the east side of the river, the Cutting Packing Company's
men were busy with their nets. They also were seineing the
river, but they were using horses to pull the seines.

It was a vivid sight, in my memory, seeing those thousands
of salmon being drawn in and the boats taking them to the
canneries.

August 12, 1895

When the *Harvester* was ready to sail, the first thing that
attracted my attention, after we had climbed the rope ladder
that hung over the side of the vessel, was a strong iron cage
containing three year-old Kodiak bears. These bears were
being taken to San Francisco for the Golden Gate Park.

We were shown our stateroom, and our grips were placed
inside. We ate before the bark sailed. Mother didn't eat much,
because she was feeling a little seasick already and knew it
would get worse, as it had on all her previous voyages.
Immediately after the meal, Mother went to bed.

The sails were being adjusted, the anchor hoisted, and the
Harvester started out on her long voyage.

Over the Waves

There was a moderate breeze for a while, but as the hours
rolled by the wind became harder, and the ocean was getting
rough. It was then that Mother got really sick.

She went through all the stages of seasickness during this
voyage. There was only a day now and then when the seas
calmed appreciably, and after a while Mother would be able to
come out on deck for a short time. When the weather was
roughest, we were all sick, sometimes not going to our meals,
but through it all Agnes and Grace took care of Mother,

cleaning up the vomit and keeping cold, damp towels on her forehead around the clock.

Sickness seldom got Mother down to the point where she didn't get up out of bed when she made up her mind to do so. This was especially true when she thought someone else needed help. All my life I have never heard her complain about her own lot. She once said, "When I start feeling sorry for myself, I just think of how much worse off others are." Her whole life was spent helping others.

But this seasickness made her more helpless than anything she had ever had. How thankful we all were when we landed at San Francisco, and her seasickness was over.

A Cagey Cook

After a meal, I often went on deck to watch the cook feed the bears. The cook generally did this himself, and the bears were always waiting and watching for him to come with their food.

One day the door to the cage got open, and the bears got out. The sailors took to the rigging and hollered to me to get out of the bears' way. The bears weren't after anybody, but the sailors were scared.

When the cook learned what was happening, he said, "I'll fix that," and he came out of the galley with a lot of food and started throwing it in the pen. The bears came back and went right in, and the cook closed the door.

Beauties of the Sea

There were times when the wind was blowing quite a gale, and the sea was covered with skeletons of Portuguese men-of-war. These tiny bonelike boats were oval shaped, about two inches long, with a thin bonelike structure running lengthwise through the center and above the hull. Their color was sky blue. There seemed to be millions of these in spots, and the wind would pick them up from the tops of waves and blow many aboard the bark.

There were many sea birds—sea quail, sea pigeons, sea doves, different varieties of sea hawks, and others that looked almost identical to our land birds, except they had webbed feet. I wondered how many land birds had their counterparts on the vast ocean.

We saw the goonies—beautiful birds with their slender, graceful wings spreading 10 to 12 feet.

The sea gulls quit following the *Harvester* after the second day and took up with a revenue cutter going north.

Many sharks were around the bark at times, some 12 to 15 feet long, most smaller.

We saw several droves of porpoises swimming by. The sailors said the wind would soon change and would then come from where the porpoises were swimming. This seemed to be true.

Corbett and Sullivan

There were several men passengers aboard who spent a lot of time in heated debate about prize fights and prize fighters. The hottest topic of discussion was the coming fight between John L. Slullivan and Big Jim Corbett. Most of the men seemed to think Jim Corbett didn't have a ghost of a chance.

Mother was seasick in her stateroom, but she could hear the loud arguments in the cabin. She said to Father, "Ernest, I wish those men would quit talking about John L. Sullivan and Jim Corbett over and over. Can't they think of something else to talk about?"

A Fine Romance

The Captain and Father were talking in the cabin about Humboldt Bay and the principal towns there—Eureka, Arcata, and Fields Landing. The Captain said, "I used to sail over that bar very often in years past. Stopped at the towns and took on lumber and shingles, Fields Landing among them. One incident I shall always remember:

"I got acquainted with a nice looking, intelligent country girl of Norwegian parents who operated a dairy farm. She invited me to their home. While I was there, the girl's mother brought in a large pitcher of buttermilk and poured a glass for me. I drank it, and then another.

"The mother raised the pitcher again. I remonstrated. She said, 'You just as well drink all you can. We're only going to feed it to the hogs anyway.'

"I cut my visit short, and that was the last of that courtship."

A Bad Dream

We awoke as the *Harvester* was nearing the Farallon Islands off the Golden Gate. The morning was bright and the sea calm as I got up and dressed for breakfast, but there was something bothering me. I told Mother, "I had an awful dream last night, and it bothers me."

Mother asked, "What was your dream?"

I said, "I dreamed Aunt Bertha died last night."

Mother replied, "Don't think about it any more. Of course there can't be anything to it."

Through the Golden Gate

We ate breakfast, and when we went on deck we saw several vessels ahead of us nearing the Golden Gate. Tugs were hooking on and towing them into San Francisco Bay.

A tug came our way. A bargain was struck between the tug's Captain and ours. A hawser was thrown to the stern of the tug and made fast to the cleat, and we started through the Golden Gate for a dock in San Francisco Bay.

The author, age seven, born in Humboldt County, California; his infant sister Ruth, also born in Humboldt; and his sisters Agnes, age five, and Grace, age four, both born in Kodiak, Alaska (taken in Eureka, California, in the winter of 1892-1893; photo courtesy of his youngest sister, Helen Roscoe Burnell, age ninety-four).

CHAPTER 19

THE LAST WORD

Billy's Cork Legs

When ashore at San Francisco, we went once again to the Windsor Hotel. Father had a lot of things to attend to on his agenda.

One of the first was to look up Billy Bailey's home and deliver $250 that had been taken up at Wood Island in a collection to help him buy cork legs if satisfactory ones could be made. Otherwise he was to use the money for whatever would do him the most good.

Father took me along, and I think Billy was happier to see Father than to get the money, as bad as he needed it.

Maritime Law

Father then went up to the North American Commercial Company's office. We had just reached the office, and Father was talking with the president of the Company when the phone rang. It was one of the previous owners of the *C. P. White*. It seemed he was angling to get the schooner back from the North American Commercial Company if he could.

The president said, "Here's a man from Wood Island with us right now. He knows all about the circumstances of the discovery and salvaging of the *C. P. White*. I will put Mr. Roscoe on the phone, and you can talk to him."

Father told the man how the ship had been found floating upside-down and how the Company's steamer had put a line to her and towed her to Wood Island where she was righted and her dead buried. The man asked for a lot of details that Father was able to provide.

Father handed the phone back, and the Company's president said, "You know, according to international maritime law, the party that fastens a line on a derelict and tows her to port is the owner of that vessel from then on." It was not a question but a statement of the fact that the North American Commercial Company was the legal owner of the *C. P. White*.

Perquisites

As Father was leaving the Company office, the president said, "Any things you want to buy to set up housekeeping, or anything else, just let me know what they are, and I will get them and send them to you in Humboldt County for just what they cost us for our Alaska trade."

I can remember Mother making out a list. Among the many items was a fine Singer sewing machine, which cost only $13.00. Father got a $75 shotgun for $15.00, and the other articles were in the same proportion. I now suspect that our prices were even lower than the Company's costs.

Extrasensory Perception?

Father went to Oakland to deliver a lecture at the 5th Avenue Baptist Church, concentrating on the development of the Baptist Mission and the orphanage on Wood Island.

He stayed in Oakland for a few days to visit the Parkhurst family and give more lectures. As I have said, the senior Parkhursts had crossed the plains with Grandfather Roscoe's first wagon train in 1852, and it was during Grandfather's second crossing to California that my Aunt Bertha was born in 1861, two years before Father.

While Father was visiting the Parkhursts, they received a letter from Grandmother Roscoe in Upper Mattole telling them that Father's sister Bertha had passed away the day before the *Harvester* had landed at San Francisco. The funeral had already been held.

When Father returned to our hotel in San Francisco, the first thing he said was, "Bertha is dead."

Way Out of Town

Several branches of the Parkhurst family had homes in the East Bay area, and they had all insisted that we visit them before returning to Humboldt County. We took the ferry and then the train to downtown Oakland. I believe it must have been 7th and Broadway.

We had to wait at the station for Wales Morgan, a Parkhurst nephew, to come with the milk wagon and take us "way out of town" to his mother's house at the head of Lake Merritt. Idella Morgan had lots of land, and her brother had land that joined hers. They operated a large dairy and sold milk in Oakland.

We stayed at Idella's and visited all the Parkhursts for two or three days until Father's brother-in-law, Frank Hough, came with his wagon and took us out to his ranch at Lafayette on Walnut Creek. We stayed there a couple weeks while Father made several lectures around the bay.

I was ten years old by the time we got passage back to Eureka on the steamer *Pomona.*

Wrangletown

When we returned to Humboldt County, we stayed in the Clark house on Summer Street again and visited friends and families in the Mattole Valley until Father accepted a teaching job. It was with the Freshwater School District, about five miles east of Eureka. We lived along the Freshwater-Kneeland Road near its intersection with the present Old Arcata Road, and the school was located at a place called "Wrangletown."

Finally a Brother

Mother was pregnant again, and on July 12, 1896, when I was almost 11, my first of four brothers arrived. He was named Stanley Boughton after the famous African explorer and my Great Grandfather Roscoe who had died four years earlier.

After Stan, Ernest and Ida Roscoe were yet to have Helen Marguerite, my fourth sister, on May 14, 1898, and then Milton Ernest on July 14, 1902; John Philip on March 24, 1905; and Robert Kenneth on September 26, 1906.

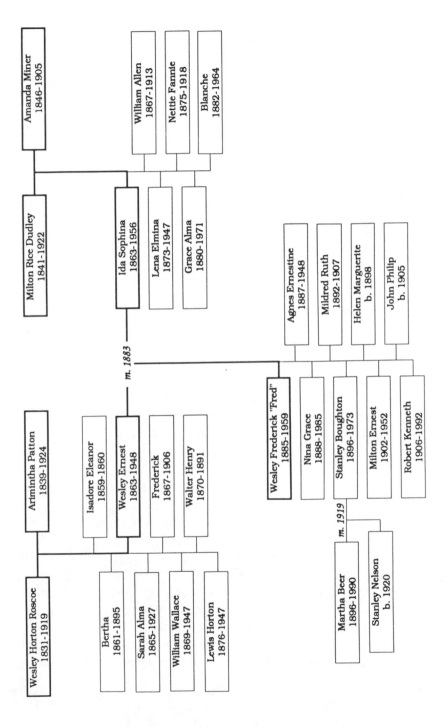

The immediate family of Ida, Ernest, and Fred Roscoe.

Another Tragedy

During the time Father was teaching at Freshwater School, Mother was corresponding regularly with Mrs. Greenfield. In one of her letters, Mrs. Greenfield told of the sad ending of Captain Bowen. He had gone on "just one more" fur trading expedition, and his schooner never returned. He left at least eleven half-orphan children.

The Final Outrage

A little later, the Greenfields came to San Francisco for a vacation and were planning to visit us in Freshwater during Father's vacation time and take a trip to Mattole over the mountain roads and along the beaches.

Mrs. Greenfield was very close to Mother, of course, and her letters were enthusiastic about the coming trip. She had been raised on a ranch in Lake County, a short distance south and a little east of Humboldt County, and the two counties were much alike in many respects.

About the time we were expecting the Greenfields, Mother got a letter saying Mr. Greenfield's plans had been changed and they would have to return to Alaska immediately, but they would be able to come down again next year and would visit us then for sure. They would be sailing north with Captain Thomas, another of Mother and Father's old and warm friends.

Soon the San Francisco newspapers reported a steamer foundering at sea. It was Captain Thomas's ship, and the Greenfields' names were listed among the missing. Little Bennie, the youngest boy, was found in the hold among some barrels, the hold filled with sea water. The rest of the family had been washed away. Harvey Greenfield, the oldest son, had been left in San Francisco to attend school and was the only surviving member of the Greenfield family.

Evidently they had been caught in a terrible storm, as Captain Thomas was found lashed to the steering gear, his eyes picked out by sea gulls.

The Last Word: Mother's

Father was still teaching at Freshwater when the Klondike gold rush started in 1897. Father got word that John M. Vance, the wealthy owner of the Vance Redwood Lumber Company and many other valuable properties, wanted Father to contact him the very next time he could come to Eureka.

On the following Saturday, Father went to Eureka and ran into Vance walking down F Street.

Vance said, "Mr. Roscoe, I want you to go back to Alaska. You have been over a large part of it and know the country. You go back and go into any kind of business that looks promising—outfitting stores, grubstaking prospectors, in fact, anything where you see an opportunity to make a big profit. I will furnish all the money, you tend to the business, and we split 50-50."

Father was raring to go, but Mother put her foot down, and we stayed in California.

Ernest Roscoe (upper right) and his students at the Garfield "Little Red Schoolhouse" in Wrangletown on Freshwater Creek near Eureka, California, in 1897. From left to right, **Front row**: Ada Foster, Lizzie Lolax, Pearl Littlefield, Mary Spinas, Hannah Anderson, Marie Coeur, Eddie Anderson, Ruth Roscoe, Della Pankey, Glenna Hodgkins, George Ferguson, Harvey Littlefield, Ray Cole, Clarence Renfroe, August Ekbum. **Second row**: Lena Anderson, Grace Roscoe, Hilda Anderson, Belle Littlefield, Ida Foster, Amanda Foster, Agnes Foster, Norris Ferguson, Earl Shields, Harvey Bjorkstrand, Glen Littlefield, Roy Hodgkins, Murray Sargent, Henry Steinberg. **Third row**: Barbara Godfrey, Wendla Lolax, Martha Bjorkstrand, Mary Godfrey, Effie Getchell, Bert Bassford, Garnet Simmons, Lou Bassford, Charlie Littlefield, Fred Roscoe, Jack Murry, Nels Bjorkstrand, Charley Lambert, William Lolax. **Top row**: William Beauchamp, Eddie Steinberg, Ellsworth Getchell, Charlie Renfroe, James Murry, Hugh Young, Charlie Beauchamp, Willie Anderson, Francis Sundfors.

INDEX

Abbott, Granville S., ed. *Pacific Baptist*, xi
aconite, an extract from common monkshood, 71
Adams, Rev. H. E., old-time revival evangelist, 98-99
Afognak Island, northeast of Kodiak Island, xii, 33-34, 36, 116, 124
Alaska Commercial Company (A.C.C.), xiii, 6, 13, 16, 18-24, 51-52, 65, 72, 109,
    113-114, 138, 153, 165, 175
"*Alaska, 1894-1895*," pamphlet of the W.A.B.H.M.S by Mrs. James McWhinnie, viii
Aleut Chief, leader of Kodiak and Wood Island Native Americans, 62, 77, 153, 157
Aleuts, Native Americans of southwestern Alaska, 13-15, 19-21, 50-51, 59, 61-64,
    70-72, 75-76, 110, 113, 134, 138, 157-158, 162
Allen, Jerry, student in first American school in Kodiak, 5
Allen, Mary, sister of Jerry Allen, 74
Allen, Mrs., Creole helper in Roscoe home, mother of Jerry and Mary Allen, 41
American Baptist Historical Society, Valley Forge, Pennsylvania, 30
American Russian Commercial Company, Wood Island ice business, 102, 113
amputation, amputating, amputee, 85, 175-176
Anderson, (Andresoff) Peter, murderer of McEntyre, viii, 6-7, 52
Angie, infant daughter of Mushwa and Scottie, 158, 161, 182-183
Arcintee, an old Indian (d. 1893), 39-40, 77, 120-121
Bailey, Billy, shipwreck survivor, amputee, 175-176, 194
baptism, baptizing, 94
Baptist Mission Reserve, patented government land, Wood Island, 107-108
barabara, 75
Barlin, Mr., supt. Cutting Packing Company, Karluk, Kodiak Island, Alaska, 185
baseball game, 4 - 5
bathhouse, steam, 70
beaches:
    Humboldt County, 87-88
    Kodiak, 2, 60
    Wood Island, 124, 154, 135, 139, 157, 164
Bear, U.S. revenue cutter mastered by Capt. Mike Healy, 125, 176, 178, 180
bears, 32-36, 47-48, 55, 58, 72, 167, 188-189
Belew, Dr., A.C.C. "doctor" and fur trader, 23
bells, cast in Kodiak, 112
berries, 39-40, 120, 132, 156, 161, 177
Bertha, steamer mastered by Capt. Hansen, 19, 51-52, 54, 77, 165, 169
bidarka (baidarka), skin kayak, 31, 113, 167
birds, 56, 96, 139, 190, 198
Blodgett, B. D., A.C.C. storekeeper, longshore boss, 21-22, 24, 69, 114
Blodgett, Mrs., wife of B. D. Blodgett, 12, 114
boats, 111, 113-114, 170, 152, 170, 184, 187-188

THE LIMESTONE PRESS

ALASKA HISTORY SERIES

DISTRIBUTED BY

UNIVERSITY OF ALASKA PRESS
1st Floor Gruening
University of Alaska Fairbanks
Fairbanks, AK 99775-1580
Telephone: (907) 474-6389
Telefax: (907) 474-7225

23. Dorothy Jean Ray. **ETHNOHISTORY IN THE ARCTIC: THE BERING STRAIT ESKIMO.** Articles. Early trade, the legendary 17th century Russian settlement, the history of St. Michael, Eskimo picture writing, land tenure and polity, settlement and subsistence patterns, place names and Tr.. of Russ. accounts of the Vasil'ev Shishmarev expedition (1819-1822). 280 pp., illus., maps.

24. Lydia Black. **ATKA. AN ETHNOHISTORY OF THE WESTERN ALEUTIANS.** 1984. 219 pp., illus. Prehistory, ethnography, 18th century foreign contacts, early Russian voyages, and biographical materials.

25. **THE RUSSIAN-AMERICAN COMPANY. CORRESPONDENCE OF THE GOVERNORS. COMMUNICATIONS SENT: 1818.** 1984. xiv, 194 pp., illus., index, notes. Tr. from manuscript material in U.S. National Archives.

26. **THE JOURNALS OF IAKOV NETSVETOV: THE YUKON YEARS, 1845-1863.** 1984. 505 pp., illus., maps. Tr. by Lydia Black. History and ethnography of the Yukon and Kuskokwim regions of Alaska.

27. Ioann Veniaminov. (St. Innokentii). **NOTES ON THE ISLANDS OF THE UNALASHKA DISTRICT.** 1985. 511 pp., illus. Tr. from Russ. ed., St. P., 1840. A classic account.

28. R.A. Pierce. **BUILDERS OF ALASKA: THE RUSSIAN GOVERNORS, 1818-1867.** Biographies of Alaska's 13 forgotten governors, from Hagemeister to Maksutov. 1986. 53 pp., illus.

29. Frederic Litke: **A VOYAGE AROUND THE WORLD, 1826-1829.** Vol. I: TO RUSSIAN AMERICA AND SIBERIA, 1839-1849. Tr. from French ed. (Paris, 1835) by R. Marshall; with a parallel account by F.H. Baron Von Kittlitz, Tr. from the German ed of 1854 by V.J. Moessner. 1987. 232 pp., maps, illus.

30. A.I. Alekseev. **THE ODYSSEY OF A RUSSIAN SCIENTIST: I.G. VOZNESENSKII IN ALASKA, CALIFORNIA AND SIBERIA, 1839-1849.** Tr. from the Russ. ed. (Moscow, 1977), by Wilma C. Follette. Ed. by R.A. Pierce. 1988. 130 pp., illus., maps.

32. **THE ROUND THE WORLD VOYAGE OF HIEROMONK GIDEON, 1803-1809.** Tr. with intro and notes by Lydia T. Black. 1989. 184 pp., illus., maps.

33. R.A. Pierce. **RUSSIAN AMERICA, 1741-1867, A BIOGRAPHICAL DICTIONARY.** Data on over 600 Russian and foreign statesmen, explorers, administrators, and skippers, Native leaders and women. 560 pp., illus.

34. A.I. Alekseev. **THE DESTINY OF RUSSIAN AMERICA, 1741-1867.** Tr. from the Russ. ed., Moscow 1975. 340 pp. A comprehensive history.

35. **RUSSIA IN NORTH AMERICA.** Proceedings of the 2d International Conference on Russian America, Sitka, Alaska, August 1987. 1990. 527 pp., illus.

36. Katherine Plummer, ed. **A JAPANESE GLIMPSE AT THE OUTSIDE WORLD, 1839-1843. THE TRAVELS OF JIROKICHI IN HAWAII, SIBERIA & ALASKA.** Adapted from a translation of Bandan. 1991. 182+94 pp., illus.

37. Rhys Richards. **CAPTAIN SIMON METCALFE, PIONEER FUR TRADER IN THE PACIFIC NORTHWEST, HAWAII AND CHINA,** 1787-1794. 234 pp., illus.

38. Lydia T. Black, **THE LOVTSOV ATLAS OF THE NORTH PACIFIC OCEAN, COMPILED AT BOL'SHERETSK, KAMCHATKA, IN** 1782. Tr, with introduction and notes, by Lydia T. Black.

39. E.O. Essig. et al. **FORT ROSS, CALIFORNIA OUTPOST OF RUSSIA. ALASKA, 1812-1841.** Reprint, Quarterly of the California Historical Society, Vol. 12: 3, San Francisco, September 1933.

** numbers not listed in series are unavailable or out of print.

Editorial Office

THE LIMESTONE PRESS

P.O. Box 1604   c/o History Dept.
Kingston, Ontario   University of Alaska Fbks.
Canada K7L 5C8   Fairbanks, Ak 99775